TO

WHAT

END

TO
WHAT
END

REPORT FROM VIETNAM

WARD JUST

PublicAffairs

New York

Portions of this book have appeared in *Harper's* magazine.
The lines from Harold Pinter originally appeared in "'Pinterism' Is Maximum
Tension Through Minimum Information" by Charles Marowitz, *New York Times
Magazine,* October 1, 1967. Copyright © 1967 by The New York Times Company.
Reprinted by permission.

*Book design and composition by Mark McGarry, Texas Type & Book Works
Set in Monotype Dante*

Library of Congress Cataloging-in-Publication Data
Just, Ward S.
To what end : report from Vietnam / Ward Just. –1st ed.
p. cm
Originally published: Boston : Houghton Mifflin, 1968
ISBN 1–891620–77–0 (PB)
I. Title
DS559.5 J88 2000
959.704'3—dc21   99–059742

FIRST EDITION
10 9 8 7 6 5 4 3 2 1

For Cameron, Evan, and Lucy

The desire for verification is understandable, but cannot always be satisfied. There are no hard distinctions between what is real and what is unreal, nor between what is true and what false. The thing is not necessarily either true or false. It can be both true and false . . . A character on the stage who can present no convincing argument or information as to his past experiences, his present behavior, or his aspirations, nor give a comprehensive analysis of his motives, is as legitimate and worthy of attention as one who, alarmingly, can do all these things. The more acute the experience the less articulate the expression.

HAROLD PINTER

CONTENTS

FOREWORD

TWENTY-FIVE years after the fall of Saigon, the Vietnam of the war years seems a vanished and discredited civilization animated by obsessions worthy of Melville. The circumstance that begat the struggle—the cold war—has vanished. The personalities that drove it—Ho, Kennedy, Johnson, Nixon, and their advisers—have vanished, mostly. All the soldiers are middle-aged or older, and many are dead. The memoirs have slowed. Of the Americans, only McNamara and Kissinger continue, self-consciously, to brood out loud. Yet the ghosts remain at the table, rising whenever Washington contemplates a military adventure. Nicaragua, Grenada, Panama, Somalia, Haiti, Bosnia, Serbia, and Kosovo, were all seen through the shadow of Vietnam. For American statecraft, the legacy is as profound as that of World War II.

In the victorious nation, some of the old landmarks endure, the hotels and restaurants of Saigon, the tunnels of Cu Chi, the rubber plantations, the sampans on the Perfumed River in Hue. The rain forest has reclaimed the battlefields, leaving only relics, the hulks of tanks and helicopters, rusting weapons, mines and bombs, ordnance that will remain lethal for a hundred years. Bones still leach to the surface at Verdun and Stalingrad, and so too at a thousand places in Vietnam. To Vietnamese Communists of the older generation, the struggle was life itself. It was a kind of soul-struggle and heavenly mandate at the same time. When the writer Stanley Karnow asked General Giap how long he was prepared to go on fighting, the great commander said—ten, twenty, fifty, a hundred years. As long as it took to win, regardless of cost. The price was high, two million lives; but it was paid. Had it been higher by twice, the Vietnamese would have to dig a little deeper. And they would not hesitate, for what was at stake was the noble ideal of unification, and freedom to pursue their totalitarian dream. A friend of mine once described perversity as a situation that enlisted your curiosity while discouraging your understanding.

There's something fantastic about the state of affairs today. With the resumption of diplomatic relations, Vietnam has become a tourist destination for Americans, many of them former soldiers or civil servants who saw duty in the war. Journalists return by the hundreds. It's possible for an intrepid traveler to visit the Ia Drang Valley or the Bong Son plain, much as old soldiers and their descendants visit Omaha Beach and Bastogne; and it is possible to inspect the fortifications at Dien Bien Phu, where the French came to such grief in 1954. The countryside is lovely and the beaches superb. Three or four thousand dollars buys you a golf package: begin your round at the links in the Saigon suburbs, then motor by air-conditioned van to Dalat and Vung Tao, golf all day long and dine nicely in the evening. So Vietnam is becoming a normal country, with all the capitalist apparatus of a normal country, the Internet and cell phones, entrepreneurs and bankrupts. You could think of it as an Asian Czechoslovakia, except you won't find Vaclav Havel. Vietnam is *sui generis*. It will proceed in its own way in its own time, when it has breathing room and the blessing of the free market and its enforcer, the International Monetary Fund. Doubtless among the old soldiers there will be some nostalgia for the time, a generation and more ago, when Vietnam was not a normal country. Their savage civil war commanded the attention of the world. Their heroic efforts brought down an American president and excited the imagination of revolutionaries everywhere: One, two, three, many Vietnams. A pity Che Guevara did not live to share the victory. Not a small thing at all for a tiny nation ever on the margins of history. That abnormal time was the time when *To What End* was written and published, and it is the time to which I will now return, with a mixture of relief and dread.

To What End was my first book, written in the west of Ireland in the summer of 1967. It had to be written at speed because the war was changing, becoming more violent even as Lyndon Johnson was promising "no wider war." On January 30, 1968, the North commenced the Tet Offensive, which was the beginning of the end for the Americans—not militarily but psychologically. Everyone knew our intelligence was defective; no one knew it was blind. When the book was published in the spring of 1968, American attitudes had shifted decisively; it was a different audience than existed the previous summer. The question "Can this war be won?" had been replaced by "How bad is it?" I had no intention of writing history, only to convey the startling ambiguities of the war and the country, the bizarre relations among Americans and between Americans and Vietnamese. I thought the war was slipping beyond irony to tragedy. A narrative could be written later but in 1967 the story seemed to have no spine. So if you could not summon Rembrandt, you could at least summon Picasso in the fullness of his cubism—she has three eyes, and the nose is hitched just below the ear.

The title was a problem. I wanted to call it *The Gook Dog That Hated Gooks and Other Stories About Americans in Vietnam*, thinking it had a nice balance of craziness and mystery. But Anne Barrett, my editor at Houghton Mifflin, thought it unwieldy, perhaps not entirely reflective of the material. "It sounds like fiction," Mrs. Barrett wrote, "It even sounds rather like a book for children to anyone who doesn't stop to think what a gook is." She had her own title, *To No End*, from a line of Thucydides in his history of the Peloponnesian war. "They suffered no small sacrifices to no end." This title was stunningly apt but I resisted, unwilling to make so bleak a judgment. The war was clearly in stalemate, a tragedy at hand but—to no end? None at all? I think now that I had somehow failed to understand what I myself had written over eighteen months of personal witness and later in Ireland. I wanted to leave the door open a crack, and so insisted on the tepid *To What End*, without even a question mark. This was a failure of nerve, and it is no mitigation to report that I was encouraged by friends at the *Washington Post*. They believed I had an enviable reputation for "even-handedness" and "moderation" and "reliability" and all the rest, a reputation that would be damaged by a title so blunt and polemical, so—unforgiving. As I say, a failure of nerve, though three decades later I can take some sly comfort in the knowledge that the war was not "to no end" for the Vietnamese running things in Hanoi. The common soldier, his widow, and his orphan, would have another view.

From the earliest days it was obvious that the Vietnam war was something new in the modern American experience, a war fought along ideological lines—the lines drawn by the cold war—and not for any reason of imminent danger to the national security, or even in support of an historic ally. In the beginning it wasn't even a war but something they called "counter-insurgency." Successive American administrations insisted that fundamentally it wasn't about Vietnam at all. It was about Communist expansionism. It was about dominoes tumbling to Singapore. It was about the Soviet Union and what the Red Army would do in Europe if the American army failed to hold the line in South Vietnam. Our allies would have reason to doubt our word and resolve (not that they were much interested in an Asian war themselves). Yet the Congress was divided. The American people showed no great enthusiasm. As a consequence, it became something of a balancing act for a correspondent to find a trustworthy angle of vision, a place in the sun where you could see as much of the action as circumstances allowed, trying always to keep the whole in mind so that you didn't exaggerate the parts. Military machines are wasteful and fundamentally error-prone, a principle as true for the Viet Cong as it was for the Americans and the ARVN, but you were not an eyewitness to the blunders of the other side. You wrote to your audience whether you wanted to or not, and it was obvious the war was not popular in the United States. Your task was not to make it more popular or less popular but to report what you saw and heard faithfully and completely. But from the beginning, Irony was the voice of choice, and irony is the enemy of faith. "We had to destroy the village in order to save it." The American soldier seems to have said this without irony, but that was not how the American reporter heard it; and so it acquired a double edge.

THERE HAD always been tension between American officials and the correspondents of whatever nationality (the French were particularly distrusted since, to the French, irony is a sacrament), and while that tension eased during my time in the war, it had not disappeared. I think of us now as a kind of school, like the Frankfurt school of criticism in Germany between the wars, or the neo-realist novelists in Italy after Mussolini. It was only a feature of the times and our employment that our métier was war correspondence. We were conscious of our independence, and conscious also of breaking new ground, and not entirely unaware of the founding fathers—Murrow for the broadcasters, Hemingway for the writers. I thought that their wars were altogether tidier and more serious than mine. But Murrow and Hemingway were antiques in 1967. Certainly Hemingway in Spain thirty years before was not the model. Much as one admired his politics, propaganda was still propaganda. Mine was the war where you sympathized with your countrymen even as you doubted the wisdom of their actions, and the cause for which they fought. Of the planners in Washington there was general contempt (and the anti-war protesters were not much admired, either, at least by me). They knew very little of the reality of things on the ground and their arrogance expanded to meet their ignorance. This view was general, not only among correspondents but among many military and civilian officials as well. So there was some common ground among the field hands. Our great task was to assemble a reliable estimate of the situation. Was the revolution gaining ground or losing it, and was the American army and the Saigon government equal to the challenge? When General Westmoreland looked at enemy dead after an engagement and remarked that Vietnamese did not have a serious regard for human life, was he correct? And if he was, what did it mean in the effort to break the enemy's will to fight? I spent many hours in the field investigating this question, to no good conclusion; so I began to concentrate not on their morale but on our own.

My own morale was high. I enjoyed the work, though as the months passed I was conscious of searching in a dark room for a black hat that wasn't there. I wondered how it would be to commit yourself to a cause. I never had, and certainly the Stalinists in Hanoi were not candidates. I confess that I believed in the power of prose, of action loyally described. You were loyal to the material. To fudge it or slant it—still less to ignore it—was a kind of sin. It was unforgivable. The effect of your prose could be helpful or not, but at least your words could be depended upon. I thought that as belief systems went, it was as good as any; at any event, it was what I had. For a time, near the end of my tour in Vietnam, I believed I had disappeared into my work—the rabbit in the magician's hat.

When Martha Gellhorn arrived on the scene in 1966, writing for *The Guardian* (Manchester), I took her to lunch in order to learn how things were in Spain in 1937. I thought if I learned about alpha, it might help me understand omega, or perhaps my role in omega. Martha had a beautiful memory and was not shy about sharing it and the more she talked about life in Madrid with Hemingway— they were married a few years later—the more envious I became. Martha in her slacks, Hemingway in his beret. I admired her conviction and shirty nonchalance and high good humor as she talked about the bombs and shells raining on Madrid and Barcelona, the difficult circumstances of daily life, the constant danger and the days without food and, no less alarming, drink. The lovers believed in the cause of the Spanish people, believed in it wholeheartedly and without reservation, and supported it with words and deeds and eventually money. She spoke warmly of their many Spanish friends, causing me to reflect that I had no Vietnamese friends, except my translator, Vu Thuy Hoang. Instead I had sources—army colonels, spokesmen for this command or that, bartenders, the concierge at the Caravelle, journalists, girlfriends of colleagues. Later, I read some of Hemingway's correspondence and found the straight reporting superb and the propaganda embarrassingly bad. His novelist's conscience—what he called his shit detector—prevented him from writing convincing agitprop. Martha's work was gorgeous, clear-eyed with the facts straight as rulers.

She went on to talk of the marvelous morale of the American army in Europe in World War II. She believed all good officers had a gaiety about them, and this had a good effect on the troops. She had the feeling that in Vietnam the Americans were frightened all the time. Officers always wore their helmets. They seemed nervous. Was this so? Sometimes, I said; and then I got the idea that I should be defending my army as she defended hers. Not often, I went on, retailing one brawny anecdote after another while she smiled gamely. When I finished my imitation of Ernie Pyle, she said she was off to visit another hospital the next day. She was writing about civilian casualties and the horrors of the provincial hospitals. I said nothing. Martha Gellhorn was one of the premier war correspondents of this century and if she wanted to spend her time in hospitals as opposed to the front, that was her business; but I thought it an awful waste of talent. Later, I decided she was on to something and decided to spend a day or two looking into the matter. And when I finally visited one of the appalling hospitals it was in the company of Prime Minister Ky and his wife and, naturally, the piece ended up being more about them than about the casualties but the casualties were included.

Martha hated the Vietnam war with all the indignation she could muster, and she mustered quite a bit, even in the weeks before her death at eighty-nine in 1998. She wrote that Vietnam was the only war she reported—and she had reported virtually every war, revolution, coup, and insurgency from the Spanish Civil War to Panama— "from the wrong side." This was not helpful. It was no more helpful than the judgment of the German mystic Walter Benjamin, who believed that newspapers in their carelessness and frivolity sought to replicate the medieval scholastics' view of the omnipotence of God. "He could alter even the past, unmake what had really happened, and make real what had never happened."

Thus, o'er the ramparts we watched.

VIETNAM was a country of dark beauty, both the landscape and the remote villages. In the highlands the land seemed to step away in five shades of green, and nothing moved on the horizon. The country seemed to be asleep, as empty as any wadi in Arabia, yet out of the range of eyesight the land was teeming, people and wildlife in a primal state. The villages were constructed of hardwood, wonderfully austere, lyrical in their vertical shapes, stilted houses placed just so, one to the other. If they had been poems, they would have been haiku, stirring an emotion that you felt but could not explain. The rhythms of these villages were slow-moving, patient, somehow outside of time. The war was distant. I believed that such a people had their own sense of the great density of things, and how offensive it was to nudge fate or to try to alter the natural order. I had no idea what that natural order was but I believed they knew, and that I was not a part of it, and that in these villages they were the ones who counted. I was an intruder, a foreigner who arrived unbidden into the neighborhood with a camera, a notebook, a deadline, and oh-so-friendly intentions that concealed sinister intent. The villagers were always hospitable while revealing little of themselves. Sooner or later I would be gone, back to wherever I had come from, and they would remain.

My days were crowded, fraught, often hilarious, sometimes dangerous—and in the aftersilence of a military action, with the body bags gathered around the command post like bundles of laundry, heartbreaking. In whatever warp of time the Montagnard villagers were living, my time was surely the leading edge of the modern world, time collapsed, time accelerating, time directed by forces only dimly apprehended but the effect invariably ambiguous and inconclusive. I spent my days making notes, and then revising the notes into a coherent "piece," one that would be read by the Secretary of Defense in his office and the milkman on his coffee break. We inhabited four zones of reality, the first three being the American version, the Saigon version, and the Hanoi version. The Hanoi version of the progress of the war was taken less seriously than the others because in 1966 and 1967 their leaders were out of sight; they did not invite you around for a drink at the end of the day to discuss the coming offensive. You had their statements, written with all the clarity and insight and candor that you might expect in a propaganda document prepared in Vietnamese by Marxists and translated into English by bureaucrats. The propaganda of the American and the Saigon government could be tested against your own experience, and everyone liked a drink at the end of the day.

And there was the situation as it was actually, the fourth version, but no one knew precisely what that was, and this was not owing to lack of effort or ingenuity or some failure of critical intelligence. Frivolous and careless are not the words that come to mind when discussing those who were trying to make sense of the war, yet the consequence could be as Walter Benjamin proposed. Unmake what really happened, make real what never happened. The inversion was accidental because the fact was this: No one knew the truth of things, whether the tide was in or out or where on the shore we stood. A mysterious turbulence was rampant under the skin of the war, and that was beyond anyone's control or prediction, or even comprehension.

IF I HAVE made too much of my hall of mirrors—fourth versions, ironies, ambiguities, haiku, and German mystics, it's because I am reviewing my life in the war in hindsight, three decades after the memoir was written. I am trying to will myself back into the clamor of those years, the most vivid of my lifetime, yet out of reach. I cannot unremember the years that followed, nor erase their shadow. They interfere with my line of sight. In 1967 I was half the age I am today and while the young writer could not look forward with assurance, the older writer looks backward with—astonishment. Where did all these stories come from? All I have to go on is this memoir, and I read it as I would read an account written by a much younger brother or a son. Many of the stories in *To What End* I had forgotten, and many I remember are not there—not the clandestine late-night visits to the swimming pool at the Cercle Sportif, not the kindness of the nurse at the field hospital in Nha Trang, not the twelve-hour Thanksgiving dinner in the Sporting Bar on Tu Do Street, and specifically not the story of the infantrymen who wanted to shoot me dead and would have, too if his company commander had not stepped between us and motioned for me to join him. One more example of the disgraceful state of journalism: I was photographing dead Americans following a firefight on the Bong Son plain. The photograph is on my office wall today, the only good one I ever made of the war—a still life at dusk, black and white, three bodies on wooden pallets, rifles beside them, palm trees above them, a composition of appalling silence and melancholy. I never sent it to the paper because I remembered the murderous look on the grunt's face and the utter weariness of the company commander as he explained that it had been a very bad afternoon; and then paused because of course I knew that, I had been with them. For a moment the captain was at a loss. My world was in opposition to his. He said at last, those casualties were that man's *friends*.

In Ireland I had trouble letting go of my book, meaning the war, then in mid-passage. The war had been my life, and I had no regrets, but it was time to turn to something else. When it came time to publish, I happily published, though I knew I would return to the subject again and again. These many years later, I have little to add to *To What End*. Probably there should have been more on the Saigon government, that thin coat of paint on the listing hull. Probably there should have been a section on American statecraft, peace feelers, bombing halts, cloak-and-dagger in Geneva, and mysterious negotiators in Paris. But we paid little attention to statecraft. Statecraft was Washington's affair, and they were welcome to it. Of course the war was unwinnable. It was useless to fight the Vietnamese. They would have fought for a thousand years. The vast, humid, unquiet land of Vietnam was a leviathan that swallowed everyone up. These many years later I believe that for too many of us Vietnam was like Herman Melville's doomed whaling ship, adrift "on a masculine sea," our university. It was a privilege to have been there.

AUTHOR'S NOTE

I was *Washington Post* correspondent in Vietnam from December, 1965 to May, 1967. All the material in this memoir dates from that time. The book was written in Ireland in the summer of 1967, and published by Houghton Mifflin the following March. This edition contains the original text. Nothing has been changed or omitted.

WARD JUST

INTRODUCTION

THIS BOOK was written mostly in Ireland, a country which I felt would be in every respect the reverse of South Vietnam. Friends who have read the manuscript tell me it has the tone of a late-night confessional. The thanks for that, if true, must go to O'Shaugnessey and some of the other regulars at Glin. Also the tipster at the Ballybunion dog track who did not want to hear about Vietnam, and advised me to keep the book short. "You're well out of it," said he.

The book is not a history, nor is it an exposé. It does not tell how the United States came to be in Vietnam, nor how it should go about getting out. It is a description of the atmosphere and of some of the events I saw in South Vietnam from December, 1965, to May, 1967, when I was there as correspondent for the *Washington Post*. There is no attempt to write a diplomatic or military history of the war; that can be more usefully explored from Washington, and someday probably will be. The view from Washington makes a different book from this one.

The book has no particular chronological order, and I have deliberately refrained from assembling an index. The point of view is mine, from Saigon and some of the other places in Vietnam, and the war is regarded within a Vietnamese-American context.

There are four abbreviations used: MACV (pronounced mack-vee) is American military headquarters, the acronym of the Military Assistance Command, Vietnam; ARVN (pronounced arvin) is the acronym of the Army of the Republic of Vietnam; USAID (pronounced use-aid) is the Saigon branch of the Agency for International Development; JUSPAO (pronounced juss-pow) is the Joint U.S. Public Affairs Office.

W.S.J.
Glin, Ireland
Washington, D.C.

1

SAIGON AND
OTHER SYNDROMES

SOUTH VIETNAM was the same, winter and summer. There were monsoons during both seasons, and in January and February in Saigon you could set your watch by the onset of the three o'clock rain. There was some change of temperature in the northern provinces, but in the south it was always hot. The heat was wet and close, and made you feel as if you were wrapped in a dripping blanket. It was so much a part of living in Vietnam that it was rarely mentioned. On nights when the temperature dipped below seventy-five, the Vietnamese would pull on sweaters and complain of the cold. In the air-conditioned offices of USAID and JUSPAO Vietnamese girls would wear heavy clothing over their filmy *ao dais*. It is best to remember that everything in Saigon and in the Delta south of Saigon took place in the heat.

The city was unique, a combination of Vienna in the 1930's, London in the 1940's, and Algiers in the 1950's. The war, an East Asian theater of the absurd, gave the city its connection with the 1960's. The war seemed to rock along without plot, rhyme or reason. The tension and vitality that war brings to any city was not from Hemingway and Orwell, but from Pinter and Beckett.

The first impression was the city, and the long, low descent over the twisting tributaries of the Mekong, the canals and watery fields of the Delta shimmering off to the south, the jerry-built shacks of the refugees on the fringes of town, Tan Son Nhut Airport itself in the heat, and the fighter planes stacked on the runway along with the Boeing 707 jets of the commercial airlines.

The traveler arrived in one of the big planes, staring out the window, the engines roaring, silent inside, after a day and a night from New York or Washington. There were the dregs of a cup of coffee, or a Bloody Mary, and bad nerves from listening, since Guam, to the rock and roll of the Supremes, the trio from Detroit, piped from special transistorized tapes through a stethoscope-like apparatus that fitted into both ears like gum and blotted out everything but the roar and heave of the engines. Fingers became a fist and tapped on the blue padded armrest, until the throb of the music became one with the plane. It was the velocity of both that brought the traveler into Saigon and the war, face pressed against the cabin glass:

> *Baby, baby*
> *Whenever you're near*
> *I hear a symphony*
> *Each time you speak to me*
> *Baby, baby*
> *Whenever you're near*
> *I hear a symphony*
> *Baby, baby*
> *Whenever you're near*
> *Baby, baby*
> *I hear a symphony.*

Down, and a shudder as the engines were reversed. The traveler exited into bright sunlight and the odor of jet fuel, and walked one hundred yards to the low white building with the signs in the inexplicable language. There were Americans everywhere. Soldiers were sprawled sleeping in the dirty terminal, which was chaos except for a small nook on the west side where Vietnamese passengers waited patiently for their Air Vietnam flights to Quang Ngai or Pleiku or Phan Rang. There was the interminable wait while immigration officials wrestled with the blue passports bearing the unpronounceable American names, and then a five-mile drive through the clogged streets to the hotel. The streets were jammed even by Asian standards, the city hung over with a heavy blue pall from the exhausts of ancient cars and Japanese motorbikes, a Honda-heaven, as someone called it, Lambretta-land. The old Peugeots and Citroëns driven by men in white suits, the delicate ladies with parasols, were relics of another Saigon. The Vietnamese drove as though crazed, thrusting the tiny yellow-and-blue taxicabs around the three-wheeled pedicabs and embassy Mercuries with skill and audacity. They yielded only to the brawny, menacing Americans driving U.S. Army two-ton trucks, who expected all civilian traffic to halt and make way. Finally everything ceased and the cars sat idling, clumped in fat, thick bunches at traffic lights. It was impossible to catch anyone's eye. All the eyes were turned inward, looking backward. The sense one received was of a heavy city, bloated, disheveled, peopled by ghosts. The Vietnamese at the side of the road, on bikes and walking, were tightly contained, wrapped in a cocoon of privacy.

At Le Van Duyet Street a young girl on a black Solex motorbike attempts a traverse from the center of the street. She does not look to the left or the right. She keeps her dark eyes on the handlebars and one hand on her conical hat, and moves across the traffic, which avoids her or halts abruptly. The exhaust on the pavement is thick and the girl has a sheer white scarf across her mouth. She makes no hand signal, no sign to indicate her passage. She simply turns the wheel of the black bike and moves, her *ao dai* gently fluttering in the breeze, back stiff, eyes set. She turns, and starts slowly up the street.

Squalor gives way to two-story American villas with lawns and white concrete walls and armed guards close to the center of town. At Duong Pasteur Americans in shirt sleeves appear on the street, walking with determination. MACV headquarters, a three-story French villa with a forest of antennae and sandbagged bunkers, stands around the corner from Marie Curie lycée, the most fashionable girls' prep school in Saigon. And at the center of town itself it is the Americans who are hurrying, weaving their way through the crowds. The Vietnamese wander, stopping to chat and buy a bottle of Bireley orange soda from cornerside vendors. The Americans rush, long-legged and sweating, impelled by urgent business. They tower over the Vietnamese, and sometimes in their hurry and impatience they place both hands on fragile oriental shoulders and gently ease bodies out of their way. Finally there are the beggars and the crippled, the tipsters and the bar girls, off-duty American infantrymen, Vietnamese businessmen, and young ARVN lieutenants, of Tu Do Street. Tu Do had been called the Rue Catinat under the French but President Diem decided, as part of a general campaign of de-Frenchification, that the street needed a new name. He called it Tu Do, which means freedom.

The airport route gave intimations of what the rest of the city was like, away from Tu Do and downtown and the handsome villas of Cong Ly Street. The slums grew out from the central city, away from the core. Unlike the large American metropolis, the core of Saigon was a haven for what remained of the Vietnamese middle class, those who had not rented their houses to the Americans. Saigon slums, swelled by the refugees, grew on the outskirts, vast accretions that proliferated as inevitably as coral, a hut at a time, each more squalid than the last. The slums were geographically linked by fetid canals, commercially dominated by Chinese merchants, and largely disregarded by an indifferent Saigon government. The American aid mission had other preoccupations, so Saigon grew as the war grew. There was nothing to be done about it. By mid-1967 the war had thrown up a vast urban proletariat which lived precariously on the fringes of all the large cities; in a year and a half, Saigon's population rose from two to three million (according to the most reliable estimates). The refugees, cut loose from their village moorings, from their ancestral graveyards, the *dinhs,* and the hierarchy, drifted aimlessly in a bewildering and hostile environment. Families splintered and farmers became cyclo drivers and girls left home to work in the American bars, or as waitresses or laundresses on the American bases. This was said to be an inevitable concomitant to the war, and for the moment a tolerable (and inescapable) price to pay for the fight against Communism. Strangely, the Viet Cong did little to exploit the situation. They, like the Americans and the Saigon government, concentrated on the villages. No one was very happy about the refugees, but no one saw very much that could be done about them. They were very low on all the lists of priorities, safely forgotten in the press of more urgent business. American officials liked to contend that the refugees were fleeing Communism, and therefore could be regarded as a net plus in the war effort. But no one took this argument seriously. The refugees were fleeing the war, and its bombs. A family found its way to Saigon or Nha Trang or Qui Nhon on the basis of rumor that fortunes could be made from the Americans. You would sometimes see the refugees, singly or in families, having made their way to the center of Saigon. There, on the busiest street corners in town, they would stand hesitating and uncertain near the curb, muttering to passers-by, asking for alms, extending mahogany-colored hands and grabbing at your shirt.

IF THE refugee came from a village in the Delta he headed for Saigon because he had been told it was the capital of his country.

The city held little of the symbolic value for the Vietnamese that Rome does for the Italians or London for the British. It was the foreigners, first the French and later the Americans, who made Saigon the capital of South Vietnam. It was necessary for bureaucratic and political reasons. Educated Vietnamese, when they thought about it at all, regarded Saigon as a synthetic city dominated by foreigners and ruled by a junta of generals. They thought of Saigon as the provincial Spanish think of Madrid: a non-capital, unrepresentative, artificial. The center of Vietnamese political life was the village; everything else was bureaucracy.

Most Vietnamese loathed Saigon, or what Saigon had become, and the more thoughtful tended to regard it as the symbol of the new colonialism, with its corruption and war-dominated economy. Intellectuals often spoke of corruption as if it had been an American invention, imported to South Vietnam for the specific purpose of weakening the fiber of the people. In fact official corruption on a grand scale was always present in Vietnam, a direct descendant of the Mandarin tradition; it was only the opportunities that were now so much greater. Saigonese pointed to the bloated wages of the bar girls, the lethargy and arrogance of the civil servants, the *nouveaux riches* among the officer corps of the army, the refugees in District Nine, and saw Pompeii in its last days. They saw Vietnam collapsing under the weight of American power and influence, as any weak society is bound to do when confronted by a stronger one. To the Vietnamese it was an atmosphere of menace and when the city administration removed the tall and graceful elms from Cong Ly Street to make way for the immense American military trucks, it seemed the final bit of decay, the last links with the old days.

The remembrance of the past persisted. Very few Americans knew Saigon in conditions other than those of wartime, and tended to doubt the descriptions of deterioration under the American occupation. In some ways Saigon was no worse than Paris or Rome, or

SAIGON AND OTHER SYNDROMES

any other large city that makes a point of catering to large numbers of foreigners. The central problem, unlike Paris or Rome, was the terms of the American involvement: not quite an occupying power, but a good deal more than a mere ally, the Americans *settled* in Saigon. The ambiguity of the position—was Henry Cabot Lodge a proconsul? an adviser?—resulted in a breakdown of law where Americans were concerned. The Americans were above the law, feared and therefore largely ignored by the national police and the Saigon government, which accorded them special privileges.* One of the most trivial, but significant, examples was the license plate TN. Cars with TN plates were allowed to park in the restricted lot in front of the American post exchange in downtown Saigon, directly to the rear of the National Assembly Building. U.S. authorities were convinced that one day the Viet Cong would attempt to blow up the PX, as in 1965 they had blown up the American Embassy. The PX was the single enduring symbol of American wealth and the American way of living, a gigantic Macy's of tape recorders and cameras, pearl necklaces, bathing trunks, Scotch whiskey, Crest toothpaste, plastic ice trays, cigarettes and *Playboy*. Ordinary cars driven by Vietnamese—or cars with Vietnamese plates driven by Americans—were shooed away by rifle-carrying MP's. The TN plate also enjoyed precedence on river ferries, and excused the driver from the payment of tolls. The procedure was reminiscent of the Chicago mayor who distributed to his cronies personal cards reading: "This man is my friend." The Americans were the friends

---

* As an experiment late one night, three Vietnamese-speaking American diplomats attempted to pay a parking ticket at the 1st District police headquarters. They were not permitted to pay it. The Vietnamese official on duty appeared to regard the attempt to pay as a trick, and fearing censure from higher authority if he accepted money from an American, he steadfastly refused to have anything to do with the matter. It had never been done before. The Americans reported there was a good deal of laughter in the police station.

of the Saigon government, and while the TN plate may have been a small concession for the introduction of 500,000 American troops in Vietnam, it was a meaningful one to the Vietnamese. It was yet another layer of privilege.

The effect of the American presence could have been worse. As it was, most of the trouble did not come from the official community but from the drifters who collected in Vietnam to work for the American construction cartel, RMK-BRJ. The trouble was invariably liquor and sex, and sometimes illegal money-changing, but in these contests the Vietnamese always gave as good as they got. The effect was less ecological than economic. The Vietnamese were not soft, and the Vietnamese spirit bent but did not break. Henry Cabot Lodge devoted much of his second tour to minimizing the effect of his compatriots on Vietnam society, and it was an extraordinary achievement that the number of Americans living in Saigon stayed at about 17,000 while the troop commitment in the country as a whole grew from less than 200,000 to nearly 450,000 in Lodge's eighteen months as ambassador. MACV headquarters was eventually moved from the villa on Cong Ly Street to an immense low-slung building called Pentagon East, at Tan Son Nhut Airport, and with that began the slow exodus of colonels from the downtown B.O.Q.'s (Bachelor Officers' Quarters).

It was difficult to imagine Saigon as the pearl of the Orient so beloved of travel writers. The villas were large and handsome and there was a zoo, a cathedral, a river and expensive shops and decent hotels downtown. But it was not a city of rhapsody. Perhaps in comparison to Vientiane, Luang Prabang or Phnom Penh, it had a certain sleazy Gallic charm; but those were not exactly five-star standards. When Vietnamese spoke of the collapse of Saigon, what they meant was the loss of sovereignty and character, and in another sense of virginity. They spoke of the three thousand years of Vietnamese history and culture and how these were being subverted by the gauche and rude Americans. But examples of this superior culture were scarce, and even the most sympathetic observers were cautious in their estimates. The arts did not flourish in South Vietnam. Painting, for example, was either florid and photographic or pastoral and imitative of the French Impressionists. *Kim Van Kieu,* the Vietnamese equivalent of *The Song of Roland,* was not highly regarded by scholars, except as an interesting myth charmingly rendered. There were no Huckleberry Finns, Fausts, or Classical Books of Odes in Vietnamese literature; nor a Lao-tse or Confucius for metaphysics. Her heroes were warriors like Cong Ly or tigerish female saviors like the Trung sisters. Music was derived from the Chinese; sculpture, to the extent that it existed at all, was Cham. When the Vietnamese spoke of their four thousand years of Vietnamese history and culture what they really meant was their way of life. But through all those four thousand years their way of life, more often than not, was war.

So the city yielded up its soul to the Americans as it had done to the French. Some of the old symbols remained, but they were fragments of a French civilization: the opera house, now the building of the National Assembly, white-domed and vaulted with electric fans and birds careering in and out of the wide open windows; the sporting club, *Cercle Sportif,* once stiff and formal but now reminiscent of a down-at-the-heels plantation house in the Mississippi Delta, the old retainers dismissed and the house occupied by Snopeses. There was a *club nautique* and the race track at Phu Tho. The old-timers spoke of the excellent food, classical French cuisine, at the Guillaume Tell and L'Amiral, and the special atmosphere of Cholon, the Chinese quarter of Saigon. These all remained, now with a Yankee admixture. Many of the signs were now in English, and there were MP's on Tu Do Street and colonels in the pool at the *Cercle.* The American symbols tended to be fewer and uglier: Pentagon East, the hangars and modern morgue at Tan Son Nhut, traffic lights, and concrete B.O.Q.'s in Cholon. The traffic lights were the main American achievement.

The town, punch-drunk as it filled up with people, reeled from month to month. The Continental Palace Hotel retained its Humphrey Bogart air and a guidebook described the Caravelle as the *ne plus ultra* of modern Indochina inns. The old-timers fed on memories: of tiger hunts in Kontum and bird shoots in Camau, weekends at Cap St. Jacques, leisurely drives through the mountains to Dalat, water skiing on the Mekong. In remote parts of the country, village elders still thought that Ngo Dinh Diem was president, or that the French still ruled.

PLENTY of tourists came to look at the war. They were army generals and diplomats from Washington, congressmen, American mayors (Sam Yorty made so many trips to Vietnam his critics grumbled that Los Angeles was the only city in America with a foreign policy), newspapermen, novelists, social scientists, baseball players, movie stars, businessmen on the make, doctors inquiring into civilian casualties, students working in the provinces, and the foreign observers: British parliamentarians, Spanish internists, Israeli generals. The standard tour for visitors was three weeks, enough to journey to Hue and speak with militant Buddhist monks, or to the Central Highlands to watch the shooting, or to undertake an automobile drive through the Mekong Delta. Three weeks was sufficient time to learn the ambiguities. One's attitudes depended a good deal on what expectations one brought to Vietnam. It was no trick to find the facts to back up the impressions, or the preconceptions: facts were everywhere, and with suitable discrimination could be used to support almost any argument. One visitor thought the war was going well, another badly. A third thought it was unwinnable. A USAID economist insisted that the Americans were building an industrial apparatus that would make South Vietnam the Japan of the 1970's and 1980's. Another American economist looked at the war damage and declared the country was destroyed for a generation.

The war hypnotized, and those whose business it was to observe it came to regard it as a drama whose characters and plot were only dimly perceived. It was not, and never could be, a question of good guys against bad because the Vietnamese half of the equation was variable. The matter has been put with great precision by the playwright Harold Pinter, who in fact was speaking of his own plays but might well have been talking about the war, the Vietnamese, and the Americans: "The desire for verification is understandable, but cannot always be satisfied," Pinter said. "There are no hard distinctions between what is real and what is unreal, nor between what is true and what false. The thing is not necessarily either true or false. It can be both true and false . . . A character on the stage who can present no convincing argument or information as to his past experiences, his present behavior, or his aspirations, nor give a comprehensive analysis of his motives, is as legitimate and worthy of attention as one who, alarmingly, can do all these things. The more acute the experience the less articulate the expression." *

There had to be an articulate framework for the half-coherent mumblings of officials and their dramatists, and for correspondents in Vietnam this was provided in the five o'clock briefing, which was held each afternoon in an auditorium in the JUSPAO building at Le Loi and Nguyen Hue Streets in downtown Saigon. It followed by thirty minutes a curtain-raising briefing by an ARVN major on Vietnamese military activities. Correspondents showed a pass to a Marine guard at the door of JUSPAO, and negotiated a maze of corridors to arrive at an air-conditioned auditorium. The briefing began with news of civilian interest: Viet Cong terrorist attacks, a medical

---

* Quoted in the *New York Times Magazine*, October 1, 1967.

team newly arrived from Germany, a congressional delegation departing and holding a press conference at Tan Son Nhut. Then came the colonels. There was a ground briefer and an air briefer. The air briefer discussed air strikes in North Vietnam, their number, duration and effectiveness. Occasionally the authorities would display an Air Force or Navy colonel, just back from a bombing run over Hanoi or Haiphong, who would submit to questions.

The briefing was the official version of the day's events. It was most competently done. The ground-briefing colonel stood on a well-lit stage behind a wooden lectern and discussed the previous twenty-four hours of what he called Free World Military Activity. (The Free World, in South Vietnam, was the Americans, the Koreans and the Australians. They acted "in support" of the ARVN's who, as we shall see, belonged to another world.)

"Twelve KIA, no captured," the colonel said. "Friendly two KIA, twelve WIA. Three missions flown in support, also artillery."

"What happens now?" a correspondent asked from the rear of the auditorium. The room is not large enough to accommodate all of the correspondents, and many of them are standing at the rear scribbling notes on the printed handout. Most of the briefer's information is already in the handout. (Or, as it was, the three handouts, one each from the Army, Navy and Air Force.) Occasionally there were special handouts from a particular division or corps command. And of course there were often handouts from the Australians and the Koreans, not to mention the other countries which had commitments of one sort or another: the Philippines, New Zealand, Thailand, Spain, Germany.

"The operation is continuing."

"Continuing?"

"Continuing," the colonel said.

"For how long will it continue?"

"I can't speculate on that."

"Where is it, again?"

"Here"—consulting the map which is projected on a large screen behind the lectern—"it's about sixteen clicks (kilometers) west of Quang Ngai City."

"So that would be Task Force Oregon."

"It would, yes sir."

"And if I am not mistaken, that is the first time Task Force Oregon has moved west of Quang Ngai."

"Approximately."

"We have moved south of Quang Ngai on, let's see, two weeks ago last Monday. And we moved north after that attack on the air base. We have not moved west until today."*

"That is correct."

"Are the ARVN's in on this?"

"Yes, in a way."

"What are they doing?"

"They had that at their briefing."

There is a short pause, and then the correspondent goes on:

"I wasn't at their briefing."

"We cannot comment on Vietnamese operations," the colonel says, crisply. "This is the Free World Briefing. The ARVN briefing is at four-thirty. We comment on the Free World Forces and the ARVN's comment on the ARVN's."

"Well, can you do it on background?"

"We do not usually do that. Where would you be if you have

---

* This sort of question became known as the "left-handed battalion commander" syndrome. It was a function of journalistic desperation to differentiate one military operation from another. An enormous effort was made to establish a "first" or "most" or "least" in the lead of a newspaper article. It was surmised that the classic lead for the non-event of a fruitless operation would be that a left-handed battalion commander, "for the first time," led it into battle.

everybody commenting on everybody else. This is Free World. The other is ARVN."

"Perhaps on background."

"The ARVN's set up their own briefing so they could handle it fully. This is for the Free World only." The colonel pauses, then recognizes a trim, precise officer in the rear. "Ben?"

A full colonel comes striding down the aisle. "I don't see what is so difficult about it," he says. "The ARVN's comment on the ARVN's and we comment on the Free World. That is the way it is set up now."

"Well, I thought you could do it backgroundwise."

"Well, hell, what's the difference?" This from a third correspondent in a seat at the front. "Why can't it be done on background, with no attribution?"

What is happening here is that the correspondents are searching for an opening to catch the colonels in a lie, or if not a lie at least a misconception. It is a grand game, reminiscent of arguments about angels dancing on the heads of pins. None of it is of any importance. The briefing became an exercise in methodology, a means of exposing the inherent error of body counts, weapons counts, search and destroy missions which had turned left at the wrong coordinate; a meticulous search for conceptual error.

The colonel, who understood the implications of the bored accents of the correspondent, looks distastefully at the men in the chairs in front of him. Then he goes to the map.

"On background: they are here"—pointing at the map, the stick striking a coordinate—"and here."

"North and west."

"That is correct. North and west."

"Thank you. Blocking positions?"

"Yes, they are blocking. They are blocking for the American battalions."

"This is all west of Quang Ngai?" It is a correspondent who has come in late.

"That is correct."

"Thank you. What are you calling this?"

"The ARVN's call it Operation Lam Son Two. But—this is all in the handout, you know—we call it Operation Mastiff." The colonel consults his notes and speaks softly into the microphone. "It's multi-battalion."

Then he goes on to discuss the other operations that day.

The dialogue is formal, polite in an almost Victorian way. The colonels call the correspondents "Sir." The correspondents mostly call the colonels "Colonel." No one would suspect that the colonels hate the correspondents and the correspondents distrust the colonels. It is mostly a hangover from the bad days of 1963 and 1964 when the correspondents thought everybody was lying to them. The colonels believe many of the correspondents to be leftist agitators. But they are bound together by the formality of the briefing, and manage to coexist. There are even some close friendships. But not many.

The briefing was the principal source of news giving the official version of the war. It was one version among many, all of them inaccurate in the singular, but the one from which most newspaper-reading Americans received their perception of the war. From the briefing came the war story, or the front-page wire service article which began, "American pilots flew 198 missions over North Vietnam yesterday, striking rail yards, storage areas, and troop concentrations . . ." It was a bad way to learn anything about the war, either the terms on which it was being fought or the means by which it might be won. This was not because colonels were lying to journalists, but because by the time news percolated up from the battle zone it was either badly garbled or hopelessly out-of-date or both. The only consolation for the correspondents was that they knew instinctively that the versions of the war which came from Saigon were intrinsically sounder than the versions from Washington. However inaccurate and misleading the view from Saigon, the view from Washington was always more so: Washington was a mirror-image away from reality. Saigon was the source of it all. What was going on elsewhere, in Moscow and London and the other capitals, was a reaction to what was happening in Vietnam. The Viet Cong mortared an outpost at Lai Khe, a long string from the American Embassy in Saigon to the White House in Washington jerked, and there was a reaction. McNamara came for a three-day inspection tour, and by looking at his appointments list and the cities he planned to visit, you knew what he was going to hear. Would he talk with McChristian? Vann? Ellsberg? Would he go to Dong Ha?

MACV prepared for the McNamara visits by drawing literally hundreds of colored charts, each meant to show how the war was going. The civilians, amateurs to a fault, took it more casually. One high-level briefer who declined to speak with notes was confounded by a request from SecDef (as McNamara was known) to distinguish between revolutionary development and pacification. He said that the two were about the same. They were not, Ambassador Lodge broke in. So two of the highest officials in the civilian mission fell to bickering among themselves as McNamara looked on with distaste. Of course the argument was much more significant than the military briefings with their statistical certainties and quantitative measurements of progress. The American mission could never make up its mind as to what was pacification and what was revolutionary development, and that was just the trouble. These too became matters of methodology. It was a question of which Jesuit was in charge.

You were your own Jesuit in Vietnam. From the roof of the Caravelle Hotel it was possible to watch an Air Force DC–3 drop chandelier flares on the far side of the Saigon River. Somewhere there was trouble, an outpost under attack, or two patrols that went "bump" in the night—and leaning over the entrecote grille to pour another glass of Bordeaux you would ask your dinner partner where she was going tomorrow, and what she hoped to see. The girl was blond and Radcliffe and in Vietnam on assignment for magazines. In time she would come to grasp the Vietnamese condition as well as anyone in the country, but then she was a very shy girl, uncertain why she was there. She talked about the Buddhists in the I Corps, and said she was going to Quang Nam province.

She wants to talk about Vietnam, but her dinner partners want to hear about New York and Washington and the mood in the United States. There is a long dialogue about what Vietnam is doing to America, as ice cream and coffee makes its way around the table.

There is a commotion now, and heads turn to the west where flares are just appearing. There are two, four, five flares and the diners strain to hear. They are listening for explosions. The explosions come and someone nods. Yes, they are mortaring Tan Son Nhut. A wire service man quietly leaves the table to make a telephone call.

It is early enough, barely after ten, so following a drink in the NBC suite the party moves on downstairs. The journalists check the room clerk at the desk for cables, and then begin a slow crawl down Tu Do Street. The party walks across Lam Son Square in the rain, avoiding a beggar with his hat in his hand who has stationed himself under the awning of the Continental Palace. One of the girls looks at the beggar, reaches into her purse, and gives him a twenty-piaster piece. Back again across the square, dodging traffic; but a jeep crashes through a mud puddle and everybody is splashed. They watch the disappearing red lights and mutter. Son of a bitch. The Goddamned American army think they own this town.

There are half a dozen children in the wake of the party, which is now cruising past the Air France office with its advertisements of Paris, Geneva, Rome, and the Riviera. The children are asking for money: Gimme 5 P, they say, Gimme 5 P. The new girl scrambles around in her purse for change, but the others hurry on. The children are always around the Caravelle and the entrance to the Tu Do Street bar district. None of the regulars in Saigon pay them any attention. Children on the street begging for money are a part of the town, like jeeps that go splashing through mud puddles.

In the Sporting Bar the group bunches together at one end, watched closely by an American construction worker at the other end. He is looking at the American girls, pretty and round-eyed, soft hair, white skin, alive and laughing. The lights are low, as they are in all the Tu Do Street bars, and in the background, from a Panasonic hi-fi system, was music from the Armed Forces Radio Network broadcasting station. Some of the bars had television but this one only had radio. It was playing rock, in between pleas for the GI's to go to church. This was a variation on the theme of atheists in foxholes, a soft-selling singing commercial delivered in close harmony, Ink Spots-style:

> *Don't you get a little lonely*
> *All by yourself*
> *Out on that limb*
> *Without Him?*

The last is drawn out, Himmmmmmm. This follows a subtle if insistent message to the troops not to kill prisoners, and to support the Chieu Hoi (defector) program. Each defector, AFRTS noted, "means more support for the GVN, less firepower for the VC." There are also appeals to use the zip code when writing home. Half a dozen times throughout the day the station would honor the Unit of the Day. This always seemed to be a transportation or quartermaster command deep in the bowels of Saigon or Nha Trang. And the news: "American paratroopers, striking deep at a Communist base area near Pleiku, are heavily engaged tonight. Early reports say that more than fifty Communists have been killed in the four-hour-long firefight. United Press International reported that a battalion of the 101st Airborne Brigade jumped off at noon . . . "

This was background to conversation at the Sporting Bar. The place was full, the girls in residence hitching up their hip-huggers and shuffling the playing cards. They played gin rummy with the men, often stationing girl friends behind the GI so they could peek into his hand. There was no need for complicated hand signals: no GI could understand the language so the girls could cheat *en clair*. The GI's knew this but didn't mind. They flew into Saigon with three months' pay after six months in Pleiku and didn't care about being cheated; getting out of Pleiku was enough. They sat drinking beer and talking, the GI's to the GI's and the bar girls to each other. They played cards because no one understood enough of each other's language to talk.

On Tu Do Street, the bar girls were not necessarily prostitutes. Some were but many were not. Most of them had Vietnamese boyfriends who managed to keep an eye on them, either by working in the bars themselves as busboys or by arriving at curfew time on Hondas to drive them home. Some Americans felt that the girls were the principal financiers of the Viet Cong war effort, and there was probably some truth to this. The Americans were not especially fond of Vietnamese girls: their undisguised mercenary instincts were unappealing, and their language unfathomable. But mostly they were held to be unresponsive. "I told her I would give her a thousand piasters if I could screw her," went the classic GI line, "and two thousand piasters if she would screw me back."

All very cynical. But the saddest sight I have ever seen is Tu Do Street at TET, the Vietnamese New Year, celebrated by the Americans as the time to bomb or not to bomb. Traditionally at TET Vietnamese return to the village where they were born. It is the greatest festival of the year, combining something of Christmas, Easter and Thanksgiving. It is a time of fireworks and presents, of drinking and honoring family and ancestors. The bars at TET are filled with girls who have no place to go, disowned as they are for becoming courtesans to the Americans. So they sit in their hip-huggers and miniskirts and vinyl spike-heeled shoes and drink Coke, dreaming of home. No amount of attention can bring them out of it. They are deep-sad and crying with longing.

So the crowd from the Caravelle sits in the Sporting Bar and talks about the war. One of the Americans is living with a Chinese girl. They converse in pidgin French when they converse at all, and now she is wedged silently into the group at the bar, staring into a 7-Up and holding the American's hand, as he leans across her to talk animatedly to a Vassar graduate. Beer arrives, is drunk, arrives again. The construction worker edges over and wants to talk. Ignored, he retreats for ten minutes. Then he comes back again and puts an arm around one of the American girls; he says he just wanted to do it. He means no harm.

Look, we're just trying to talk among ourselves.

Haven' seen a round-eyed woman for six months, the construction man says. He is red-faced and bleary with whiskey.

Well, find one someplace else.

Who 'n hell you guys think you are?

Look, friend, we don't want to bother . . .

Snot-noses.

OK, let's go.

And the crowd from the Caravelle, all bills paid, gets up to leave. They depart quickly, in a group, leaving the construction worker behind, angry and wanting to fight. They walk down Tu Do Street, everybody agreeing that it was a bad idea to leave the Caravelle. There are so many Americans in town it is impossible to go somewhere and have a drink without some drunk bothering your girl.

Well, that ended it. The hell with Tu Do Street. It's nicer to drink at the Caravelle, anyway, and that way there are no problems. Back to the NBC suite. Edith Piaf, Charlie Byrd, and Beethoven. Room service ice. Nice.

"WE ALL lived the same," said the middle-aged woman, talking rapidly. "Ate the same food, were hungry together, took the bombs together. In the middle of the city during the siege you could hear the shell come out of the gun, and hear it hitting, usually nearby. If you were riding on a tram when it was hit, you were hit along with the people in it. There was a common danger. There was very little liquor, and the food was terrible."

That was Martha Gellhorn on the Spanish Civil War. She had come to Vietnam to write a series of pieces for the *Guardian*. Vietnam was only the latest in a series of Gellhorn-written wars, beginning with Spain and then China, Europe in World War II, the Middle East, Greece, and now Asia. Her position on Vietnam was formed before she arrived, but the atmosphere of Saigon did nothing to undermine it. She was against the war on all counts, and would denounce it to all comers. She supported an immediate withdrawal and some kind of reparations payment. She thought American policy amounted to genocide. One of her points of reference was the Spanish war. "Nothing *but*," she said when I asked her if the correspondents covering that war regarded it as a noble one. "And we knew we were right. We knew, we just *knew*, that Spain was the place to stop fascism. This was it. There was no other place."

It seemed anachronistic in the cool world of 1967, where reporters of my generation prided themselves on a professional detachment. The compulsion was to tell it like it was, even if what it was was your own country at war and the way it was, if told truthfully, was not "helpful" to the effort. There was no sense in Vietnam of a war which would halt the advance of Communism; it was simply "the Vietnam war" and to those who lived there it was a war largely without ideology, always excepting the majors, colonels and generals of the army, who did see it as a struggle between the free world and the non-free world. Because of the doubts over the legitimacy of the struggle, and the conditions of life in Saigon, a man felt vaguely like a voyeur. Part of the schizophrenia was the imbalance between the field, where the war was being fought, and Saigon, where it was being managed. The correspondent of the Washington *Post* was not obliged to live in a Special Forces Camp at the Cambodian border, or to eat C rations in a jungle for a fortnight. In Spain the correspondents felt closer to the war and less like spectators at least in part because of the common privations. It seemed to me an appealing thought, and I wondered if the reporting would be different if Saigon were under siege and bombs burst nightly in Lam Son Square, if food and liquor were scarce. Would the perception of the war be altered if there were no Sunday night dances at the Brinks B.O.Q. in downtown Saigon? Would the cause of the war seem nobler if the Saigon government and the Americans were under greater pressure? But how would Hemingway and Matthews and Martha Gellhorn have reacted if it had been the loyalists who bombed Guernica?

In Vietnam it became a compulsion to get out of Saigon and into the field as often as possible. The justification was that the countryside was critical to the winning of the war, and in part that was true. But the reasons really had to do with conscience, and the impulse to find reality. If Saigon was unreal, then the war must be real. The part of Vietnam that was straight and without corkscrews was the shooting war. It was the only part of it that made sense without qualifications. All of the arguments and the doubts became irrelevant when men fought to survive. When I would comment that the battlefield behavior of American troops was almost the only fact about Vietnam that I found admirable, Martha Gellhorn snorted and said it was a case of "just buddies." The idea was that men were not fighting for any reason, or any ideology, but because they were there; they fought for their friends.

That was probably true, for any difference that it made, but it surely did not detract from the extraordinary courage shown by the men who were there, fighting a war to no applause. Second only to safety, the mature infantryman values comfort, so after struggling through a Viet Cong minefield in the afternoon it was quite possible, indeed likely, that he would receive a hot meal delivered by helicopter to the bivouac that night. If the infantryman got to Saigon he could telephone home; some of them called from their base camps, reversing the charges. Every tiny MACV outpost in the most remote province had its supply of cold beer and English gin, and nightly Hollywood movies. This was taken along with the fighting in the jungles and paddies, which was as terrible as fighting is anywhere.

"In Spain, correspondents actually went hungry," Martha Gellhorn had said. People went hungry in South Vietnam, but they were not the correspondents. I suppose that it doesn't matter whether correspondents are hungry or not, or whether there are dances at the Brinks or English gin at the MACV compound in Camau. Every soldier likes hot meals in the field, and the Caravelle is superior in every way to a foxhole. And none of these things are crucial to whether or not the war in Vietnam is a just war or a winnable one. The nobility of the war is a matter for historians. It is enough for a journalist to report that the atmosphere in Saigon was destructive, and tended to infect.

This will be called, not without some justification, the hair-shirt analysis of the Americans in Vietnam. It is not the whole story, but it is one part of it, and because the attitudes of Americans in Vietnam were critical to the way the war was fought, it is worth pursuing. For all the good works, the money and the hospitals, the volunteer doctors, the aid projects, the dams and the schoolrooms, the truth is that it was an unequal war, and everyone knew it. There was no Viet Cong air force, let alone Viet Cong B–52 bombers, and no artillery fire bases (although in time the North Vietnamese would cause havoc with Russian-made mortars and rockets). I have no doubt that the Communists, if they had possessed the aircraft and bombs, would have used them far more ruthlessly than the Americans used them. As it was, they had tools that were much more effective in a people's war. The basic and most useful question is not and never has been the effect of American firepower on the Vietnamese—it is the effect on the Americans, who bear responsibility for its use. It would somehow have seemed more reasonable if there were convincing evidence that the B-52 strikes and the artillery bombardments at night were helping the war effort, rather than hurting it. But there was no such evidence. The Americans were in Vietnam with the most powerful air force and the finest army in the world, and they could not halt the aggression. Battles erupted and were won, but the war seemed no closer to ending; the battles seemed then like scenes in an endless play, leading from nowhere to anywhere. The fight was unequal.

What the hell does it take to win this thing? asked a general late one night. *What do we have to do to them?* He had watched that day as the helicopters brought back green body bags from the field. The bags were lumpy and heavy with the dead. The helicopter crewmen unloaded the bags and laid them side by side in the dust near the airstrip, then took off again for another load. Nearby there was a billet of Vietnamese soldiers. As the bodies were being laid out you could hear the laughter and sounds of roughhouse from the ARVN compound. Vietnamese were not impressed by death, ours or theirs, and their lives were not changed by it. The general, fighting back an awful rage, strode off in the direction of his helicopter.

SOME of the Americans would say that the trouble lay in the instinctive knowledge that they were not fighting for the existence of America, nor for any tangible set of ideals, but for a mythical

Vietnam, one which had been celebrated by Eisenhower, Kennedy, and Johnson but which did not in fact exist. This was the Vietnam of the brave, freedom-loving Vietnamese. I knew very few brave, freedom-loving Vietnamese. They had other names for it, and other concepts, but those were in a different language, literally and figuratively, which neither translated nor traveled. It was very well to speak of the loss of Southeast Asia, of a gigantic domino board whose final domino was Washington or Waikiki, but the war was in Vietnam; its justification, for those who were there, had to be in the context of Vietnam and the Vietnamese. The SEATO agreements were not persuasive arguments sitting around a tent in Kontum, and while a general could make them, and believe them, he could not get truly inspired by them. If Ngo Dinh Diem was the Winston Churchill of Southeast Asia, as then Vice President Johnson described him in 1962, who then was Ho Chi Minh? Hitler? When Diem was overthrown in 1963, he was regarded as a despot. What did that make Ho? And where then were the brave, freedom-loving Vietnamese?

The population did not engage in the struggle. The Viet Cong did not regard American weaponry as decisive. And the inequality of the struggle, 500,000 men and their machines for so little advance, only increased American frustrations. It *was* unequal, and therefore unfair. It went against the American grain. When the guerrillas bombed a billet or assassinated a district chief, the Americans called it terrorism. They had to call it terrorism because guerrilla warfare did not fit the scheme of war as they were fighting it. American aircraft were first sent out after the mortaring of the airbase at Pleiku, an attack described as terrorist in character. The efficiency of the U.S. Air Force made it inevitable that in time the air war in the North would become the principal fascination of the Vietnam conflict. It was what the Americans did best. The bombing of the North came as a direct and logical consequence of the frustrations of the ground war in the South. Now it is a war out on its own, a private war with MIG's, SAM missiles, anti-aircraft fire, Russian and Chinese ships in the Haiphong harbor, and all the rest of it. Can Hau Nghia province be pacified or the Vietnamese political process inspired as a result of a dogfight between Phantoms and MIG's over Hanoi?

But how could you change it? The war was not a tennis match, with seeds, or an auto *grand prix* with corrected times for the slower cars. You did what you had to do to win, or what you thought would bring victory closer. If it seemed that bombing a power plant in Hanoi would save the lives of American soldiers, you bombed the power plant. And if after two and a half years of bombing the war seemed no closer to solution, you did not claim that bombing was a failure. You claimed that there was not enough of it, or that it wasn't begun early enough, or that crucial targets were excused from destruction. How could millions of pounds of bombs over enemy targets conceivably be a failure? The logic was inescapable. In Vietnam a moderate was a man who thought that the only thing worse than winning the war was losing it, for what would come with defeat would be far worse than anything that would come with victory. So the war was fought, and a plausible and powerful case can be made that given the situation in 1965, all the combat troops should have been committed at once; once the interventionist course had been decided, the Americans then should have pressed ahead on a one hundred percent basis, with troop call-ups and rationing at home. But it happened piecemeal, and hindsight is an unfair tactic to use in talking about American policy in Vietnam. In prosecuting a conventional war against a skilled guerrilla army operating among, at best, an indifferent population, there was a heavy psychological price to pay. And the Americans were paying it.

A sergeant major, one of the most decorated noncommissioned officers in the army, a veteran of Europe and Korea and a line sergeant in Vietnam, talked about the Viet Cong one day at the base camp of the 1st Infantry Division. He described an action just ended, where a squad of Viet Cong had fought to the last man to hold an indefensible position. There was an escape route, but the enemy did not use it. "We had to kill every one of them," the sergeant major said. "But the thing was they stayed, even though they knew what we had. They knew we had a full company, with artillery and mortars and the rest. They fought all day, *and they knew what we had*." It confounded the rules of military logic as the sergeant major knew them. He said that he didn't care what the colonels at MACV said about the Viet Cong. "For my money, the Viet Cong is the best fighter I have ever seen anywhere. Man for man, he is as good—maybe better—than we are." Then, with no sense of irony but only saying what was true and factual, he added, "Of course, that's because he's fighting in his own country."

2

KY, THE GOVERNMENT,
AND THE AMERICANS

Prime Minister Nguyen Cao Ky's closest friend in the American Embassy in Saigon was the ambassador, Henry Cabot Lodge. Lodge was not the man he relaxed and drank with, a capacity filled by an amiable U.S. Air Force brigadier general, but he was the man Ky listened to and solicited advice from. Other Americans had other sources, but the ambassador had Ky and from that contact grew a policy. The policy was that the prime minister represented stability in South Vietnam.

In June of 1965, the generals swept aside the civilians and installed themselves in office. After twenty months of coup and counter-coup, of ineffective civilian rule and chronic upheaval, the generals mounted the seesaw and promised stability. Ky was named prime minister, the chief executive officer of the government, and Lieutenant General Nguyen Van Thieu, a taciturn infantry officer, was named chief of state, an office largely ceremonial. Though both men had participated in the coup against President Ngo Dinh Diem, neither was especially well known. Lodge arrived in South Vietnam in August for his second tour as ambassador, the replacement for General Maxwell D. Taylor, who had of course been Lodge's successor in 1964. Lodge settled in quickly and, in addition to his other duties, became an informal political adviser to the prime minister, who was the age of his youngest son. The ambassador became fascinated by the Vietnamese and their labyrinthine politics. Like John Milton, who sought to explain the ways of man to God, Lodge sought to explain the ways of Saigon to Washington. He knew many of the politicians from his earlier tour, and in time came to like Ky, particularly his candor. "He's a pilot," Lodge once said, by way of explanation. "He's brave. He's, ah, polite. If he were in school, I suspect he would do well."

And Ky liked Lodge, although he was scarcely more articulate about the reasons. After Lodge left to be replaced by Ellsworth Bunker, Ky allowed that he regarded the ambassador as the most trustworthy of the Americans. He said he consulted Lodge on personal as well as political matters, and so far as he was concerned the loss of Lodge was a loss to South Vietnam.

The ambassador, who at sixty-six had been successively a congressman, senator, chief U.S. delegate to the United Nations, and vice-presidential candidate on the Nixon ticket, felt that political principles were universal, to be applied with equal logic whether in America, Europe, or Asia. You had to understand a man's power base, who his friends were and who his enemies were. Above all, you had to be sympathetic. South Vietnam, as Lodge would remind visitors, was not a politically sophisticated country; it was at war, and people were tired. There were no democratic traditions. A government had to *govern,* had to show its authority, and for the moment the dissenters must be forgotten. Above all it would be madness to impose American standards on the Vietnamese. Unity and stability came first, and once they were established the war (which Lodge regarded primarily as a police problem) could be won. He personally was sympathetic to Ky, for—as he pointed out—while Vietnam was not awfully sophisticated, it was terribly complicated. The ambassador would name the complexities, then shrug. "How can you expect a pilot to know those things?"

The ambassador's own orientation remained American. Always skeptical of Vietnamese elections, Lodge laughed when there were charges of vote fraud in the election of a constituent assembly in September 1966. "Remember what happened to Dick and me in the South Side wards of Chicago in 1960," he reminded his aides. "What makes you think it is any different in South Vietnam?"

WHEN Ky came to power there was scarcely an informed official, either American or Vietnamese, and least of all Lodge, who thought the regime would endure. Ky seemed the antithesis of political durability in South Vietnam: he was young (then thirty-five) in a country which revered age, a Northerner (his family was from a village near Hanoi) ruling Southerners, an air force officer in a military establishment chiefly composed of infantry, a dashing, handsome, flamboyant figure, inclined to Don Juanism; informal, inexperienced, not especially popular with his fellow generals, and conspicuously unequipped with either a political vision or popular support. It was typical that Ky was portrayed in the foreign press as a daring fighter pilot; in fact, while making his way through the ranks of the Vietnamese Air Force (RVNAF), he flew two-engine transports.

"He is no Bismarck," the ambassador said in an aside generally regarded as something of an understatement, "and no Cavour either. But he's learning." In 1965 and 1966, Nguyen Cao Ky was all there was. It is probable that even the generals did not expect him to last, but put him forward at the last minute as a compromise prime minister who could easily be dealt out in the next cabinet reshuffle.

Ky had played a substantive role in the revolt against Diem (his planes flew air cover over Saigon); he had no known enemies; he had amassed no fortunes; he was personally honest. The sachems of the joint general staff, much in the manner of traditional American political bosses, were satisfied that the air vice marshal (a title Ky seems to have devised himself) would be a satisfactory symbol and, like a dish cooked *flambé,* would be colorful without doing any damage. The precise combination of forces which brought Ky to the top are not known and will probably never be known; in the early days he looked suspiciously like a front man. But Ky stuck and by the middle of 1966 it was clear that the generals were in control and that the prime minister was the symbol and principal spokesman.

What Ky was symbol and spokesman *of,* however, was a more complicated matter. The "government," if such it could be called, was a hopelessly confused and confusing apparatus. There were really three basic governments in Vietnam, four if you counted the Americans. Probably the most important of these was the permanent civil service, trained by the French and financed by the Americans, technically responsible to the generals, but in fact an independent force which worked on its own inner logic. The generals* assembled in Saigon to construct national policy and appoint ministers and, on certain occasions, the province and district chiefs. These were the colonels, majors, and captains who were responsible sometimes to the generals in Saigon, sometimes to the corps commanders. As the senior officials at the province and district level (which correspond, in America, roughly to states and counties),

---

* The generals were formally known as the Directory (sometimes the National Leadership Council), whose membership, before Thieu was formally elected president in September 1967, was ten senior officers—Thieu and Ky, the four corps commanders, the chief of the joint general staff, the defense minister, and two others whose identity shifted according to the pressures within the military.

their responsibilities were both civil and military, which meant there were connections with the civil service (principally the ministry of the interior) as well. The corps commanders were yet a third apparatus of government: there were four corps areas each ruled by a major general. In time, the Directory would relieve the most intransigent—Thi of the I Corps, Tri of the III Corps, and Quang of the IV Corps—and replace them with more tractable men. But for much of 1965, 1966 and 1967, the corps commanders, elsewhere called warlords, appointed the province and district chiefs; those chiefs, in turn, were responsible to them through the military chain of command. Standing in back of the Directory was the Armed Forces Council, which was an assembly of fifty or so influential military figures, division and regimental commanders, senior air force officers and admirals of the Vietnamese Navy.* The Armed Forces Council was consulted on matters of very high policy, and was understood to hold a veto over decisions of the Directory. The precise authority of the AFC was not clear to Americans in Vietnam.

This was the machine that Ky had to operate in order for the government to work and the war therefore to be won. The best example of the difficulty involved was the bureaucratic tangle surrounding the revolutionary development cadre program, the plan to thrust 59-man teams into the hamlets and villages of Vietnam to do good works and win the loyalty of the people to the Saigon government. The cadres were financed and trained by the Central Intelligence Agency at an encampment at Vung Tau, the Vietnamese Riviera fifty miles east of Saigon.* But they were under

---

* The Navy was said to have more admirals than ships.
* CIA men were among the ablest in the country, and there was a theory that the agency never should have allowed itself to become so deeply involved in the cadre program. It diverted talented managers, some of them fluent in Vietnamese, from more rewarding chores. Like finding out what the Saigon government was up to.

operational control of the Ministry of Revolutionary Development (MinRevDev) which was headed by a major general, Nguyen Duc Thang. Both the ministry in Saigon and the teams in the field had their full complement of American advisers. The corps commanders, province chiefs and district chiefs had their say (or "input," in American bureaucratese) as the responsible officials in the countryside. So did the American provincial representatives. It was crucial that the teams be protected from Viet Cong attacks by battalions of the ARVN, so the ARVN division and regimental commanders were consulted. The Americans at the Office of Civil Operations (OCO) wanted a say-so, and of course General Westmoreland and his civilian aide, Robert Komer, kept close tabs on the program.

The ministries in Saigon ticked along with very little interference from the generals. MinRevDev became a kind of all-purpose ministry after a while, principally because it was well lubricated with American money and because the minister, General Thang, was energetic and able. Ky and his associates on the Directory ignored most of the other civilian departments except for the ministry of finance, which was monitored because the Americans had told the generals the country was in danger of a financial collapse due to inflation. (Ky personally did not take the advice seriously. "How can there be any trouble when everyone is making so much money?" he asked.) While the generals kept a close watch on the finance ministry, they placed little confidence in its head. Au Truong Thanh, a politically ambitious economist who was minister for six months in 1966, complained that the generals would not tell him how much money they planned to spend in prosecution of the war, or where they planned to spend it. Thanh said that to be finance minister in South Vietnam was like being a male nurse in a madhouse; eventually he resigned. The other ministries continued their ambling, paper-clogged ways, fulfilling their principal function, which was the payment of small salaries to overworked bureaucrats. Ky and the generals either financed their projects informally (not to put too fine a point on it) or through MinRevDev.

Apart from the formal apparatus of the Vietnamese government, there were informal centers of power which appeared on none of the tables of organization. Brigadier General Nguyen Ngoc Loan ran the national police under rules largely of his own making. The largest labor union, the CVT, had powers above and beyond the conventional labor union (although not, apparently, the power to secure decent wages for manual laborers). In the highlands, Montagnard tribesmen lived under a kind of local option with the government and the Viet Cong. The Vien Hoa Dao, the militant Buddhist Institute for the Execution of the Dharma, was powerful enough to secure annual payments in the millions of piasters as a kind of revolving compensation for the faithful killed in Ngo Dinh Nhu's pagoda raids four years before. Perhaps most important of all, despite the military character of the Saigon government (or maybe because of it) the Vietnamese military lived entirely outside civil law. This meant that as a practical matter law enforcement did not exist in South Vietnam, since soldiers were rarely prosecuted for misdeeds—which ranged from demands for free beer to homicide. In time, the Americans would try to create a police field force to bring a measure of social justice to the suburbs and the countryside, but the project foundered at least in part over arguments about who would control it. Civil justice was really what the war was all about.

Imposed on all of this was the American advisory effort, a system of threats, checks, balances, gifts, grants and loans; of counterparts and co-signees, projects officers and systems analysts, provreps and distreps, JUSPAO and USAID, economists and agronomists, labor leaders and special pleaders, taxmen and businessmen, importers and exporters of such stupendous weight and sprawl that it threatened to collapse the entire structure. The larger the American military effort became, the greater the civilian effort to match it. The advisory effort, both civilian and military, had at length gone full circle. The language problem (among others) grew so great that the Americans who started as advisers to the Vietnamese ended up having the Vietnamese as advisers to them.

But none of this had very much to do with the population, which was not consulted on political, military or bureaucratic matters. The population showed its interest by ignoring the regime, except for a certain morbid interest in Ky who was regarded as something of an exotic, married to a gorgeous airline stewardess (not at all in the Mandarin tradition) who had inexplicably traveled to Tokyo to have her eyes surgically straightened, and had lately taken to miniskirts. These cultural notes, which were published in all the Saigon papers, would set Vietnamese of all classes and stations to giggling. There was the prime minister, in his black and white Captain Midnight flying suit, with his straight-eyed wife, *also* in a Captain Midnight suit zippered from crotch to collarbone, touring a bombed-out hamlet chucking children under chins and bantering with village elders, accompanied by the foreign press jostling and taking pictures. To this, the peasant shook his head. None of it made sense. Ky was a Martian. His northern accent was incomprehensible, so the southern peasant seldom understood what he said; and his *youth*—how could a man so young be in so great an office? There were only too many voices in South Vietnam to supply the answer: the Americans put him there. Thus Ky came to be regarded as an American puppet. People believed it absolutely because Ky was so outside the norm of experience. To the villager it was a plausible, indeed the only, explanation.

THE AMERICANS seemed satisfied. As Ky's confidence grew, they began to speak of his "stature" and "capacity for growth." There was astonishment all around at the surefootedness of the regime with Ky at its head. Lodge talked approvingly of the prime minister's reasonableness: "He listens to me," the ambassador said. In the beginning, Ky affected nonchalance. He was neither seen nor heard, and spent his days in an immense office behind a vast desk barren of paper. He could pass a ninety-minute interview with a correspondent and not be interrupted once by telephone or messenger. The single index of his title and authority was a signed Norman Rockwell print in sepia of the President of the United States, signed affectionately by Lyndon B. Johnson. In interviews he spoke earnestly of returning to the air force. Questions concerning his political future were met with a shrug. Flying was what he did best, and the nation was at war: "I am no politician," he said. "I want to get back to the air."

And it was impossible not to believe him. His manner was reminiscent of a certain type of disinterested lawyer who comes to work for the federal government in Washington. He is serious about serving the people, tithing a part of his professional life for what he imagines to be the common good, government service. He tells friends it is an interim matter, that once he gets the Senate Subcommittee on Rural Development or the White House Office on Hydroelectric Affairs straightened out, he will return to his law firm, where he belongs. That is the way it is in the beginning. But the volunteer becomes fascinated with the government and its influence, and the appurtenances of power. Power becomes an attraction; the longer he stays in Washington the less likely it is that he will ever voluntarily leave.

So it was with Ky. In the beginning he relinquished something he knew and liked, the command of the Vietnamese Air Force, for something he didn't, the Vietnamese government. In the first months he was prisoner of his own ignorance of the ways of bureaucracy and the power available to a prime minister. But as the rumors of *coup d'état* slipped into the background, the prime minister began behaving like a prime minister. He began to touch the levers of power and to the surprise of almost everyone, some of them responded. Ky men began showing up in government jobs, as province chiefs and district chiefs, and in the Saigon ministries. Ky men began to emerge as majors and colonels in the army. He would install one friend, Colonel (now Brigadier General) Loan, as chief of the national police and another, Major General Le Nguyen Khang, as commander of the III Corps.* There were well-publicized meetings with President Johnson in Honolulu and Manila, and a goodwill trip to Korea and, much later, excursions to Australia and New Zealand. By late 1966, Ky began to speak less and less of returning to the air force. Ky and his college of generals, having decided to hang together, began to regard themselves with something approaching permanence. More important, they were encouraged by the Americans. They were encouraged to behave as a government, and rule. The operative American policy was not to rock the boat. Stability was visible and growing. Saigon had a government, and it worked.

Some of the critics thought otherwise. Life is more than the absence of death, and government is more than the absence of anarchy. The trouble was that the government did not govern, it presided. Sometimes it ran the war (or at least that part of the war which the Americans were not running), but the governing—the exercise of control—was left to the civil service or to the political baronies of the corps commanders, province chiefs and district chiefs. Typically very few of these functionaries (with the exception of the

---

* These were the so-called "coup commands." The III Corps ringed the capital, and there could be no troop movements in or out of Saigon without Khang knowing about them. Similarly Loan controlled some of the major cities (at least as much as anyone controlled them). There could be no Saigon coup against the Ky regime without either Khang or Loan knowing about it. Of course, as commander of the air force, Ky controlled the skies.

corps commanders) truly wished to function. It was a clumsy and fragmented regime, neither repressive enough nor heavy-handed enough to inspire popular hatred (as Diem's regime had done), nor adept enough nor talented enough to inspire respect (as Diem's regime had also done). There was no question of the affection of the population.

Difficulties were everywhere, but chief among them was the prime minister himself, who was always more popular with the Americans than he was with the Vietnamese (either the generals or the population). I think the prime minister's influence inside the Directory was slight at the beginning but grew as his value as a symbol grew. He became a symbol of unity and a symbol of determination to resist the Communist hordes and restore decent government to Vietnam. He was helped by the American press in Saigon which became increasingly friendly, after a long period of estrangement from any part of the official establishment, American or Vietnamese. The generals knew this, and having an exaggerated appreciation of the power of the American press, sought to capitalize on it. Meanwhile, for the official Americans the very endurance of the government recommended it. The image was just forming in the opening months of 1966, and it was not an image ideally suited to firing the imaginations of war-weary South Vietnamese.

It was about this time that American officials, both civilian and military, began to talk confidently of how close the allies had come to losing the war the previous spring. It was an unusual admission. "We didn't realize it, and the press didn't realize it, but the Viet Cong almost won it in May and June," the officials told correspondents. One of the officials, a senior American diplomat, said that if the Viet Cong had been bold enough to attack Saigon, they probably could have taken it. The implication was that matters were far worse twelve months ago (that is, the spring and summer of 1965) than anyone had realized; the long haul would now be longer and more difficult than anyone had forecast. But defeat had been avoided, and with the new stable government the war could truly be prosecuted. The officials said that it was essential to the prosecution of the war that Ky and the junta remain at their posts and extend the authority of the central government. But stability must not be threatened.

Trouble was gathering in Central Vietnam, the five populous northernmost provinces comprising the I Corps.* Traditionally separatist and the most politically volatile region in the country, "the center" was quietly stirring and fomenting resistance to the generals in Saigon. The immediate objective was to gain elections for a civilian government, but underneath that lay a wide range of grievances against a regime considered illegitimate, unrepresentative, and discriminatory in its attitudes to the center. Beyond that, and not very far beyond it, was the simple belief of the snobbish, cultivated *centristes* that the generals were arrogant and uneducated, reactionary in their politics, and subservient to Washington. Buddhists led by Tri Quang, students led by Buu Ton of Hue University, politicians led by the mayor of Danang, Nguyen Van Man, and military officers and ranks led by young dissidents from the officer corps of the 1st and 2nd ARVN Divisions, were all broadly agreed on the necessity for elections. Ky himself helped set the stage with a speech late in January, 1966, promising elections within a year. But a general's promise was not good enough.

The chief government agent in Central Vietnam was the I Corps commander, Major General Nguyen Chanh Thi, an able, honest, up-from-the-ranks officer with wide popular appeal in the provinces of Quang Tri, Thua Thien and Quang Nam. Thi had never concealed his contempt for the junta in Saigon, and had been publicly scornful of his old friend and classmate, Nguyen Cao Ky. Thi, a na-

---

* Pronounced eye-corps.

tive of the region whose network of agents went very deep into the society, felt he should be left alone to run the corps with no interference from Saigon. In a confrontation late in February, Thi baited Ky over a cover story on the prime minister in *Time* magazine. Thi thought Ky had permitted President Johnson to intimidate him at Honolulu two weeks before. The prime minister, bullyragged by Thi, returned to Saigon humiliated and enraged and demanded of his associates on the Directory that Thi be sacked—either that, or the prime minister himself would resign. The Directory, ever mindful of American support and the emphasis on stability and unity, and apparently finding it convenient to retain Ky, agreed. When Ky came to Lodge and informed him he had decided to sack Thi, Lodge's first question was (in these words): "Have you got the votes?" By that Lodge meant, were all the generals in agreement? Ky replied that they were. Lodge nodded, and said that in that case, Ky should go ahead. There were differing interpretations later as to whether Ky had meant to ask Lodge's advice or whether he was informing him of a decision already made. Lodge said it was the latter.

The decision to fire Thi was of great importance, a quantum jump in the junta's political ambitions. Vietnamese political figures were stunned, aware as they were of trouble in the I Corps and Thi's popularity among the people. "Mind you," said one of the top civilian officials of the regime, "there will be no end of trouble if Thi is fired." The Americans, particularly the men in the embassy's political section, were dubious about the enterprise—although the chief political officer, Philip Habib, told the foreign press in a background meeting that he thought the government could pull it off and emerge stronger from the experience—"a gamble," as Habib would say, but if successful, desirable. The dissenters in the embassy, and most Vietnamese willing to express an opinion on the matter, regarded it as an act of terrible *hubris;* Thi was too popular, too powerful, too tough to cave in without a struggle. But Lodge argued that if Thi could be successfully removed, the warlords in the other three corps areas would then be put on notice that the government intended to govern. To bring Thi down was in a sense to bring them all down. The Americans were now going beyond mere stability to the conviction that Saigon must rule not only in the capital, but in the provinces as well.

Although Thi was popular with the American military commander in I Corps, Marine Lieutenant General Lewis W. Walt, he was viewed as a disruptive force within the Ky government itself. No one doubted his anti-Communist credentials, nor his honesty, nor his ability, nor his popularity. What they doubted, really, was his ability to function within the system. This was found wanting, and so Thi was purged. "The writ of the government has got to run in the I Corps," Lodge said. Walt was dismayed at these events, but finally he too was forced to capitulate. It was, in the end, a triumph for bureaucracy.

There was, of course, the other matter of the Buddhists. The embassy had been waiting for a shoe to fall ever since Ky assumed power. The Buddhist militants had been quiet, but there was no guarantee they would remain so. Despite Tri Quang's debt to Lodge (Tri Quang was permitted to take refuge in the American Embassy when he was on the run from Nhu's secret police in 1963), the Buddhists made no effort to keep the Americans informed of their activities. More importantly, the Americans made little effort to keep up with Quang and his associates. To many Americans in Vietnam, Tri Quang was an *agent provocateur*. There was no consensus on his ideology, but those who knew him best insisted he was no friend of the war. Others called him a Communist, but supplied no proof. One point was indisputable: to the extent there was organized opposition to the war, the opposition was centered in the ranks of the militant Buddhists. They and the generals were on two different tracks, but tracks which at some point were bound to collide.

The rebellion that followed the dismissal of General Thi will be the subject of many accounts, and the best of these will not be published until the war is ended and all the participants free to speak. The day-by-day events can be recounted, but at great cost in confusion; consult the daily newspapers for the months of February, March, April and May, 1966. It is still not known precisely who was controlling events in the I Corps or, indeed, whether anyone was controlling them. What is clear is that the Buddhists and militant students of Hue and Danang instantly seized on the Thi firing as an excuse to attack the government; they were joined by senior army officers and government bureaucrats, all of whom were loyal to the deposed commander (who retired to his bungalow in Hue, there to remain until the summer when he was exiled to Washington, D.C.). After a day or two of silence, the demonstrations began in Hue and Danang. The tone was at first mild, the demonstrators demanding no more than a reinstatement of Thi. Then the signs and posters called for elections, the resignation of the junta (or, in the rhetoric of the rebellion, the Thieu-Ky clique), the withdrawal of the Americans, and finally denounced Lyndon Johnson as an enemy of the people. The USIS library was sacked and burned, and the American government closed the consulate. There were suicides by fire, beginning in Hue and Danang and finally spreading, like the demonstrations, to the other cities of I Corps and south to Nha Trang and Dalat and finally to Saigon. The central theme became anti-American.

Americans watched that spring with a kind of horrified fascination as the situation slid to *Götterdämmerung*. The war ground to a halt in the I Corps, but persisted elsewhere with American casualties. For two months the Saigon government did not govern in the five northernmost provinces. Ky made promises, then smashed them. Tri Quang granted interviews which were by turns militant and conciliatory, and always Delphic. Ky marched on Danang in

April, then backed off. There were a succession of I Corps commanders, none of whom could bring the regular battalions of the ARVN into the struggle on the side of the Saigon government. Then, in May, a detachment of Rangers under the command of Ky's closest ally, Brigadier General Loan, entered Danang, occupied the pagodas and brought the city to heel. But not before eighty Buddhists had died, and the population become almost irretrievably embittered. Hue was sealed and it, too, gave in. These events followed the government's capitulation on the central Buddhist demand: election of a civilian government. What the junta agreed to was the election of a constituent assembly to write a constitution for Vietnam. Election of a new government would be provided for in the constitution.

The Buddhist rebellion never caught on in Saigon, and for that reason it failed to topple the government. The demonstrations never captured more than a fragment of the city's middle-class and school-age youth. In easygoing Saigon there were no real grievances against the regime: there were no Rasputins like Ngo Dinh Nhu, nor harshly repressive acts against religious groups or political parties. The Ky government was hardly seen to govern at all, and hence was regarded as more joke than threat. The claim of the Buddhists that *all* responsibility for the pagoda raids in Danang rested with the Americans, principally Lyndon Johnson, was patent nonsense, and the Saigonese saw that, too. Saigonese watched events in the I Corps with annoyance, not sympathy, and a sense that now was not the time to overthrow the government.

The Ky government had been harsh, and would argue that the country was in the throes of civil insurrection which had to be suppressed at any cost. It was regarded as a police matter, "normal," Ky said, although later he would acknowledge political overtones. The Buddhists had reckoned on a spontaneous uprising throughout the country, and had lost. Some said the loss was inevitable after the attack on Lyndon Johnson, which made it certain that the Americans would give all necessary backing to the generals. So the rebellion was crushed, and with it went a very important part of Vietnam. Tri Quang retired well into the background of Vietnamese politics, and the most militant students were sent off to prison; the rector of the University of Hue, a prime intellectual force behind the demonstrations, was jailed for a time but finally allowed to resume teaching at Saigon University. The result in the end, however, was the destruction of the only solid political force in South Vietnam, the militant Buddhists and their bonzes. In retrospect, the rebellion was probably the last chance the Americans had to keep the sympathy, or at least the neutrality, of the non-Communist leftists in South Vietnam.

Amid the wreckage stood the Americans, uncertain as usual about what it all meant, and with a war to be fought and won. American officials knew only what they were told, or what they could pry out, and that was often incomplete or wrong. When the rebellion was crushed, did it represent a victory for American policy? A defeat? Or was it a happening, irrelevant to questions of wisdom or folly, victory or defeat? The atmosphere was one of victory. "The government pulled it off," said one official. "You have got to hand it to Ky." But there was uneasiness when officials looked at the implications for the future. The war could not be fought if there was no Saigon government. If it meant the destruction of political Buddhism to retain the Ky government, and therefore stability in South Vietnam, then the Buddhists would have to be destroyed. There was abundant evidence that the Viet Cong had infiltrated the ranks of the agitators, and some officials contended that the rebellion itself was part and parcel of Hanoi's strategy to win the war. The official American view was more generous. "We know there are Communists agitating in Hue and Danang," said the chief spokesman for the American mission, Barry Zorthian, "but we don't think the movement is Communist-controlled."

The point is crucial. With the vision of hindsight, some critics have claimed that Hanoi was watching the American reaction to the I Corps rebellion very closely. These critics have held that if the Americans had shown sympathy to the Buddhists (*i.e.*, supported their demands and insisted on reform within the junta), Hanoi would have taken it as an indication of U.S. *bona fides* in the matter of a representative government in South Vietnam. The standpat American approach, so the theory went, indicated anew that the Johnson Administration was preparing a fight to the finish, a military rather than a political solution to the war. It indicated to Hanoi that the Americans wanted no part of a coalition government. Evidence of Hanoi's views is very slight. The theory rests more on instinct than on fact.

In any case, it wasn't going to happen. At the time, and the atmosphere at the time is not irrelevant, it seemed that everything would go down the drain if the Struggle Committees prevailed.* They promised nothing, no program or agenda or savior. They were reminiscent of Luddites let loose in a glass factory: joy through destruction. An American administration more Machiavellian than Lyndon Johnson's might well have pondered the possibilities of this and withdrawn support from the junta, deliberately stepped aside and let the Viet Cong pick up the pieces—or, much less likely, hoped that the Vietnamese would put together a representative regime in which the army would play a subdued role. But the time wasn't right. The Vietnamese military were not going to voluntarily step aside, and the Americans were still convinced the war could be fought and won. The battles were going well (better than they would be a year later)

---

* The Vietnamese understood, if most Americans did not, that Struggle Committee was only a loose translation. The Vietnamese word *dau tranh* implies a soul-struggle, a fight to the death for the preservation of justice, or of a man's identity. To "struggle" is to rebel with all your life-force.

and from MACV came the customary assurances of advance, once, as a division commander put it, "we can get this goddamned government glued together again." So there was never a chance that the U.S. would abandon the enterprise to the Tri Quangs. It would have been the equivalent of abandoning it to Ho Chi Minh.

Assessing the prime minister's performance, American diplomats would call it "adroit." It is an incredible adjective in retrospect, though perfectly plausible in the atmosphere of summer, 1966. It was revealing of the extent to which American policy has got itself tied to the junta and the stability that the junta, chiefly Ky, represented. Ky's performance was adroit in the manner of the drunk who pours water over himself as the house burns to the ground. But no one ever credited the generals, particularly the prime minister, with moderate politics or a sensitivity to divisions within the country, and it seems unfair to tax them, and him, with it now. The generals behaved like generals.

And Americans like Americans. Support for Ky and the junta was from then on complete. The uneasiness came in the post-mortems of the rebellion, and how the rebellion bore on American policy. If the policy was to win the war by force of arms, then support for Ky was correct—indeed, inescapable. But if the policy was to negotiate, or put together an interim government as a preliminary to seeking a political solution, then the rebellion was the perfect framework to encourage alternatives to the generals. But American policy was two-headed, both to fight and to seek negotiations, which implies a political solution. The one did not have precedence over the other, and therefore to identify the American interest became exceedingly tricky. It depended on estimates of *what would happen*. It depended on estimates of the situation in South Vietnam, and there were no agreed estimates. The principal guiding motive, it seems to me in retrospect, was morality. Withdrawing support from Ky and his associates would be stabbing them in the back. Support in the first place was partly a legacy from the years of turmoil immediately following Diem's downfall, and partly Lodge's personal conviction that the air vice marshal was a force for good, and could—as everyone put it then —"carry it off." And there were practical considerations: if Ky were jettisoned, who would replace him? The junta could presumably have been sunk without a trace during the rebellion, but there were no successors. Anarchy would have been the winner, as even the Buddhists refused to put forward a candidate and nearly every capable civilian in the country had been associated at one time or another with the discredited regimes of 1964 and 1965. There were no shadow governments in either Saigon or Hue, nor imaginative civilian leaders with both a program and followers. To withdraw support from Ky meant returning to square one, to the old years of turmoil and tumult. And for what? These were the questions to which the critics never had very satisfactory answers, except that sly smile and soft query: Do you want to get out of Vietnam or not?

Then there was the war, which endured as if there were no politics. The period of heaviest North Vietnamese infiltration was during the period of Buddhist upheaval. The American and North Vietnamese military machines ground on as if what was happening in Hue and Danang was as remote as Newark or Detroit. And when the questions were put to thoughtful American officials in Saigon, the answers always seemed to rest on points in the past:

If American support for the generals had not been so generous in the first place . . .

But if support had not been generous, the generals—or at least those generals—would not have survived, and what was wanted in 1965 was survival.

. . . if urban politics had been actively encouraged . . .

But if urban politics had been encouraged, there would have been heavy opposition to the generals, in a country already wracked with enough upheaval. It would have meant a new series of governments.

. . . if the Buddhists had not been crushed and sent into exile . . .

But they threatened the very existence of the government.

Did it ever occur to you that the generals conceivably were not the answer?

There were seven—or was it eight?—civilian regimes in 1965 and 1966. How many chances do you give them?

The United States should have forced a solution, and imposed a representative government.

Ha, ha, ha. Did you ever try to force a Vietnamese to do anything?

You are a cynic.

No. I've just lived here too long.

You have never identified the American interest.

That is for Washington to do, not me. I just live here. And fight the war. And deal with the Vietnamese. And hope I get out with half a shirt.

Choices were not made. Events shaped the diplomacy rather than vice versa. The American Embassy in Saigon always seemed to be dealing with today, never tomorrow and rarely yesterday. It barely was able to keep pace with events, almost never to anticipate them. Thi happened; Hue and Danang happened; and the Americans had been unable to influence the response of the Saigon government. Post-mortems and lessons learned were for the historians and occasionally the journalists, rarely for the diplomats or the soldiers. American policy in Vietnam was a matter of improvisation, with the single clear objective being the achievement of stability. But what came after stability? It did not take a young foreign service officer long in South Vietnam to realize how little influence Americans had on the course of events. "Of course, our hands are tied most of the time," said one of the senior policy-makers. Then, with a smile, "You have to remember, it's *their* country."

THERE were marvelous theories about the true nature of the Saigon government, and most of them sprang from the fact that its most powerful members were natives of North Vietnam. Few, if any, had been Viet Minh. They were refugees, with the contempt a refugee sometimes holds for his host country; a Southerner, to a Northerner, is languid and casual, lazy and seldom very zealous about anything. This odd state of affairs, the government in the South being run by refugees from the North, demanded some explanation, and in Vietnam the more intricate the explanation the more likely it was to be believed. Some theories were vastly entertaining. One was that a faction of the Dai Viet Party (a political/commercial/religious sect in Central Vietnam) controlled the generals, from Thieu and Ky on down. The Dai Viets in turn were working for the French secret service (everyone's *éminence grise*), which was in league with the Communists in Hanoi. Ky and the other generals worked both for and against the Americans as they worked both with and against the Viet Cong, each believing that it was exploiting the other. The Viet Cong had very close links with the French, who sought to deliver South Vietnam from the Americans and incidentally to justify their long colonial rule. The objective was to discredit the American effort, particularly the effort to secure land reform and bring social justice to the countryside. The Americans had to be taught that what was required of them was men and money, not woolly theories about Western democracy and programs drawn from Jeffersonian political tracts. The specific instance which supported the conspiracy theory was the action of the Ky government to suppress the Buddhists. Ky undertook this enterprise, according to the theory, to demonstrate that the Americans were supporting a reactionary government (*i.e.*, his own) and thus bring censure from foreign liberals. The Buddhists, controlled by the Viet Cong (or, perhaps, vice versa) of course cooperated in their own demise. It was a magnificent conspiracy in which everybody was in league with everybody else. The American embassy knew all about it, but was (in the words of the most hot-eyed advocate) "not yet prepared to move."

The fact was that the Americans did not know what the Ky government's links were, to the French or anybody else. One thoughtful American political officer was convinced that the junta's machinations would never be known until the Vietnamese themselves talked. His theory was that there were countless contacts between the Saigon regime and Ho Chi Minh's government both in the North and in the South ("Why not? They all know each other.") on a whole range of subjects, and if you had access to the correspondence and the conversations you would understand the logic of the war, at least the logic as the Vietnamese saw it. There were without doubt contacts at the lower levels, district chief to district chief and battalion commander to battalion commander (particularly when the commanders of both units were Southerners), but the Americans did not know what the contacts were about. The Americans remained on the outside looking in, fighting the war and struggling for stability.

The Vietnamese generals were often in the same position as the Americans, since few of them understood English well enough to know precisely what was being got at. They could not understand the mechanics and authority of the American press, and were baffled by the stream of comment from Washington on the Vietnam war. In a typical week there might be statements from the President, the Secretary of State, the Secretary of Defense, the Presidential press secretary, the White House adviser on National Security Affairs, and two senators and a congressman just back from a tour of the front lines. Beyond that, there were the private statements—mostly reassurances—of the ambassador. My impression was that Ky was the junta's Milton, interpreting the ways of the Americans to the Vietnamese. Privately, Ky was amused at the American pronouncements on the war. He and his associates were convinced that given the slightest opportunity Washington was pre-pared to liquidate. Confidence grew simultaneous with the American troop buildup, but the old doubts never completely disap-peared. When the troop commitment reached 500,000 men the ex-pressions of anxiety were less frequent, although paradoxically there was more alarm, now because of the raucous cooing of the doves in Washington.

Ky counseled moderation, and explained privately that Amer-icans were difficult and sought always to dominate. As his famil-iarity with the English language increased, the prime minister became an excellent and effective public speaker. Smothered and overshadowed by Lyndon Johnson and the Americans at Hawaii and Manila (subjects of acid comment in the vernacular press), he came back at the 1967 summit meeting in Guam and dominated the Americans. As participants later admitted, the meeting itself was to no real purpose (it generally served only to annoy politically-minded Vietnamese, because in their view each time Ky and Thieu met with Washington, it added a bit more legitimacy to the regime), but Ky controlled its public aspects completely and thor-oughly by the simple expedient of emotion, the tone of a man who was involved. He came on as a patriot who loved his country and was determined to see it survive. First he delivered a skillful cri-tique of American policy, carefully exposing the contradictions and curious public postures of Washington. What was to be done about the infiltration? Why were Cambodia and Thailand permit-ted to be sanctuaries for the enemy? Why were troops not sent to Laos? This done, he summoned the Washington *Post* and the New York *Times* to a midnight interview to say that there were no differences between the authorities in Washington and the authori-ties in Saigon. The interview took place at the villa put at Ky's dis-posal by the Americans. The prime minister and six friends sat comfortably drinking soft drinks and chewing roasted corn and speaking of cooperation; and laughing. The premier wanted to make it clear there were no differences between allies. But Saigon had its own views on matters involving "its very existence" and those views, for the good of all, had to be expressed. Allies could afford to speak with candor.*

Ky's final press conference at Guam was a masterpiece of controlled tension. It was an emotional appeal to the American press and public to judge him and his government fairly, and a precise and moving eulogy to the Americans and the Vietnamese who had died in the war. "We need badly, and more than any people, peace, because for years we are suffering from war," he said. "I have seen many of my friends now dying for the cause of this country. They are not only the best friends of mine, but they are the best sons of both Vietnam and America."

Reproducing the words does Ky a disservice, since they are as commonplace as prose. What made them work was the studied awkwardness of the delivery and the transparent sincerity of the emotion. The prime minister's accents are heavy, almost sullen, but that afternoon his voice halted, broke twice, and he came across with great force and great style, gripping the lectern with both hands and nervously clutching a cigarette. There was nothing synthetic about it, and Ky was seen in his essentials: an unsophisticated, patriotic man, bored by statecraft and concerned only for his country, the armed forces that served it, and the enemy that beset it. Ky had the inner conviction of the man who had been there and back, the man whose country it was and who, best or worst, would go on

---

* It was at this meeting that Ky disclosed the reason for the peculiar coincidence that in the constitution just completed there were 117 articles, and 117 words in the preamble. There were 117 delegates and the constitution was signed on September 9. The sum of the digits was nine, Ky explained, a lucky number in Vietnam. His astrologer insisted that the 117's would be fortuitous. The assembly apparently agreed.

living there and fighting the war. Americans came and left, he seemed to say, but the Vietnamese went on. The war went on. It was the most appealing moment of Guam.

This all came after statements by Rusk and McNamara, and therein lay Ky's principal advantage: he succeeded middle-aged men with tired, avuncular arguments and trivial observations. Ky that day was a welterweight outclassing wrestlers. When he finished there was silence in the officers' club on Nimitz Hill, the site of the press conference. Then, touched by sincerity, correspondents applauded.

Guam happened after a series of oral disasters which would have destroyed a prime minister of any other country. Lodge periodically lectured Ky not to speak to the press as he would speak to his cabinet, or his wife or, presumably, Lodge himself. It was doing Ky no good, and Washington was upset. It was giving the prime minister a bad image abroad, the image of carelessness and warmongery. Questions were raised in the British Parliament and the U.S. Senate. The *New York Times* was hostile. People regarded him as a war lover, a flamboyant eccentric militant who would plunge the world into holocaust. Why did he continue to talk of an invasion of North Vietnam, and "dealing with" Red China? Lodge counseled restraint, but Ky shrugged off the complaints, probably because he knew he said nothing in public which American generals did not say in private and, as a practical matter, his government controlled the local press and therefore could censor any indiscretions affecting internal affairs. As for the foreign press, what did it matter? It was wise to keep foreigners on edge, and every time he made a controversial statement he was given solicitous attention by the American Embassy. Any head of state so closely involved with the Americans was sensitive to the charge: American puppet! So Ky would make certain that there was no mistaking his loyalties.

The prime minister used to talk of his "realism" about South Vietnam. His realism was that if the Americans were not prepared to obliterate North Vietnam, then they had best prepare for a long war. Without going into the implications of "obliterating" North Vietnam, it seemed a sensible and reasonable enough observation. It had the ring of accuracy. To Americans who felt he should make at least an occasional bow toward negotiations or amnesty or a coalition government, he replied that South Vietnam was too fragile for that. He would recite the figures of Viet Cong terrorism. At the slightest hint of a softening position, Ky said, his armies would refuse to fight—on the basis that if peace was to come, it was senseless being killed in the last battle. He viewed the South Vietnamese Army as the last best hope of a nation weary of war. He felt that the army had been the only force which had prevented a collapse in 1965. He had the military man's contempt for civilians, and particularly civilian solutions. Ky viewed Southern politicians as so many rabble, the first to run at the sound of gunfire and the first to propose surrender. He had, as an American friend said, the mentality of an army colonel. His anti-Communism was straight from Fort Leavenworth (where he had trained as a young pilot), couched in the phrases of the National Indignation Convention or Billy James Hargis, except that for him, the Communist conspiracy began in Hanoi, not Moscow or Peking. In a way part of this had to do with civilians, with soft solutions and nebulous groupings of irresponsible, quarrelsome politicians. In the prime minister's view, the civilians were no more trustworthy than the Communists: they had proved it with the bickering in 1964 and 1965, when the country was nearly overrun. They did not love the country, they loved power. Ky would admit to other faults, but not the fault of insufficient patriotism. And he felt that other military men agreed: the soul of Vietnam was to be found in her battalions.

It was a morale factor. Ky seldom spoke of negotiations, with the

North or anyone else. "No!" he once cried at an airport press conference. "Never with Communists!" The National Liberation Front, he felt, was not representative of anything. To those who thought that negotiations were the salvation of the American position, Ky's statements tended to put his government in a bad light. But Ky looked at it from Saigon, not from Washington or New York, and it seemed to him that negotiations were not useful. If you were a militantly anti-Communist air vice marshal born in North Vietnam, trained at Leavenworth, and none too certain of the future, there was no other position to take.

THE PRIME minister was passionately anxious that the Americans believe him honest. This was a state so rare among Vietnamese officials, particularly generals, that it was a real credit; and as far as I know, it was never disputed, even by Ky's enemies. The prime minister lived quietly in a bungalow at Tan Son Nhut Airport entertained by Western movies from the United States, cockfights, occasional evenings on the town at Maxim's or La Cigale, flights in his World War II-model Skyraider fighter plane, and weekend trips to Dalat. Dalat was the Tuxedo Park of Vietnam, a cool hide-away in the mountains 200 miles north of Saigon where generals and businessmen kept villas, and the Viet Cong kept out of sight. The finest French restaurant in the country (some said in all Indochina) was La Savoisienne, until the proprietress, Madame Grillet, closed its doors with the complaint that business was bad. Dalat was strictly Vietnamese, having been put off-limits to American troops after a series of incidents early in 1966. Ky and his wife, Tuyet Mai, would go to Dalat with friends for the weekend, and hunt tigers or elephants and practice target shooting with a pair of pearl-handled revolvers. Ky loved to hunt, and would spend two or three days in the bush stalking game. The security services were not happy with this arrangement since the Viet Cong controlled a good portion of Tuyen Duc, the Dalat province.

Ky had a kind of *blitzkrieg* honesty about himself and about Vietnam that made him the most engaging of men and the best of interviewees; there was no taboo subject. He declared the bungalow off-limits to politicians, stating that if he had to see them in his office he didn't see why he had to subject himself to them at home. Mai, disliking the politicians, was pleased by that. "Never believe what any Vietnamese tells you," Ky once said, "and that includes me." He reckoned that in Vietnam "eighty-five percent of all rumors are true." At the height of the Buddhist crisis he once turned innocently to a reporter who had asked him for an estimate of the situation and shook his head. "Trouble? There is no trouble in Vietnam." Seated comfortably in the rear of his reconditioned DC–6 (he continued to angle for a jet, arguing that every other head of state had a jet, so why not he), he would light a cigarette and talk for two hours about corrupt province chiefs, North Vietnamese infiltration, his troubles with the Americans, and the pleasures of flying an airplane. He rejected the notion of anti-Americanism in Vietnam, partly because for political reasons he was obliged to, but mostly I think because he appreciated more than anyone the extent of the American sacrifice. He was unwilling to believe that this went unnoticed by the bulk of Vietnamese.

He could not keep a secret and in the early days he gave the American Embassy fits with his habit of off-the-cuff unrehearsed commentary. The most memorable of these occasions took place a few nights before the election of a constituent assembly in September, 1966. It was a reception at the bungalow in honor of the prime minister's thirty-sixth birthday. Two little children romped on the helicopter pad as a sixteen-man band played Hawaiian music. White-coated waiters passed beer over ice, and stiff canapés were available at a long table on the lawn. Near the bar, Deputy Prime

Minister Nguyen Huu Co,* recently returned from a seventeen-day swing through Europe and North Africa, was lecturing American correspondents on the high price of lobsters in Paris. Co talked easily and reporters listened to him or interviewed each other, waiting for the prime minister and his wife to appear. It was a well-attended affair, with all the principal figures of the regime on hand: RevDev Minister Thang, Information Minister Tri, Cabinet Secretary (later ambassador to Washington) Bui Diem, Vietnam Press Chief Linh, as well as an assortment of generals and colonels and ministry officials.

The officials were as anxious as everyone else for the prime minister to appear, for that afternoon substantive comments had been made. Substantive comments were always being made, but these were more substantive than usual. They were recorded at two locations, mainly Tay Ninh where Ky had gone to commune with the Cao Dai leaders. There were stories, all sorts of stories, about new invasions of the North, about Ky running for the presidency, about Ky visiting the United States, about Ky fearing a terrorist attack on his home (it came later that night, about a dozen rounds of mortar fire), about two Frenchmen who had paid fifteen million piasters to the Viet Cong to sabotage the election now only four days away. There was an attack on General de Gaulle in which the operative phrase was, "For many years I've not paid any attention to what he says."

The journalists were waiting for confirmation or denial, and the

---

* Co was one of the authentic cranks of the Ky regime, and surely the richest. Willowy, light-haired, fast-eyed, he was minister of defense as well as deputy prime minister and his business activities (or, to be accurate, those of his wife) were said to reach deeply into all sectors of the Vietnamese economy. There was talk of import licenses and certain defense contracts, and charges of graft and profiteering were often made, but never proved, although a number of attempts were made to prove them. Co was forced to leave the country early in 1967, and is now in exile in Hong Kong, living—according to the reports—very stylishly.

officials were looking for deeper meanings. It says something about Ky or about journalism, perhaps both, that it didn't make any difference what he said; none of it represented a new policy, or a new act, or even a new gesture. What it meant was more excitement, another quotation added to the growing Ky file, a headline, a new squiggle on the political lie detector—and laughter. Mostly laughter.

When Ky appeared, gliding from the interior of the bungalow, a wise smile on his dusky face, nodding with Miss Mai on his arm, walking on the balls of his feet, it was clear that he was preparing another virtuoso performance. He was instantly surrounded by the press, who began with pleasantries about the weather and the beauty of his wife. Ky was being offhand, casual as usual about the statements of that afternoon. The journalists wrote quickly in small notebooks, peeled off to refill cocktail glasses, and then returned to rephrase the question.

An Indian journalist, who looked and spoke like a diplomat, was leading the inquiry into the possibility of the survival of a civilian government and the chances of a Ky candidacy when the question of the presidency went before the nation. Was it true . . . was it not true . . . did not the prime minister think . . . would not the prime minister say . . .

Eventually Ky tired of it all. He said that of course if he were drafted by the military he would run. But it wouldn't happen. Nguyen Van Thieu, the senior man and chief of state, would run. And the prime minister would support him. Anyone could see that.

"But Thieu told the newspapers he wouldn't run," said the Indian.

"He wants to be coaxed," the prime minister said, incredulous that anyone actually in the newspaper business could take journalism seriously.

"But . . ."

"He'll run," Ky said with a smile, "he'll run."

And nine months later, that is exactly what happened. Ky made an abortive and inept try for it, but at the end the generals pushed him aside. Whether for reasons of youth, or impetuosity, or immaturity, or simply on the basis of likes and dislikes, no one knew. The Directory, led by Thieu, decided that the Armed Forces Council should make the choice. And they decided that the senior man, who happened to be a Southerner as well, should represent the battalions at the polls. His support evaporating, Ky stepped aside and accepted the vice-presidency. It is difficult to draw a moral, other than the obvious one that in Vietnam events are not always what they seem. In any case, the Americans supported the military decision. Bunker himself acted as mediator between the now-estranged Thieu and Ky. Of course they won the election, and stability in South Vietnam acquired a new face.

3

SOME REFLECTIONS
ON PROGRESS

A SOLDIER came to Vietnam in January of one year and left in January of the next, a twelve-month tour. Before the war became a serious war, that is, until sometime around the middle of 1966, most officers looked on the tour as an opportunity to advance their careers and apply their training. It's the only war we've got, they'd say; most of the diplomats and the journalists agreed with them. Some of the civilians had elaborate theories about being where the action was, about not understanding American life in the 1960's without first understanding the Vietnam predicament. But few looked on Vietnam as a permanent assignment, and even fewer made a genuine effort to understand the Vietnamese. The civilians, including the journalists, were no different in this respect, except that they tended to stay in the country a little longer. MACV mathematicians and psychologists described a soldier's efficiency curve as precisely as a missile's parabola, concluding that the first three months were new and strange and efficiency therefore low, the middle six months filled with activity and bustle and efficiency therefore high, and the final three months preoccupied with home and family, and staying alive; the situation in Vietnam was unchanged and efficiency therefore low. There was criticism of the twelve-month tour, but General William C. Westmoreland defended it as necessary, indeed vital, to morale. As the war dragged on, officers increasingly came back on a second or third tour. These were some of the ablest men in Vietnam, but there were not nearly enough of them. The principal criticism of the twelve-month tour was that it tended to institutionalize impermanence. Men in Vietnam were transients, traveling salesmen of war and democratic processes.

Combat is the *sine qua non* of soldiering, and every professional soldier knew that his career depended to an extent on his behavior under fire. There are a few American generals who never commanded a rifle company in combat, but not many; and no chiefs of staff. The medal that is worn above all the others is the Combat Infantryman's Badge. For the career man, combat is *the* essential experience—both as a man and as a soldier. If the experience was muffed, if it all went badly, the shock could be devastating. If it all went well, if the officer proved to be both brave and resourceful, all things were possible. They were more possible in the "line" than anywhere else, and the logic became inexorable: captains wanted companies, lieutenant colonels wanted battalions, colonels wanted brigades, and major generals wanted divisions. This was where the action was, where the test would come. The professional soldier arrived in Vietnam with both enthusiasm and ambition.

For captains, majors and lieutenant colonels assigned to advisory posts in the districts and provinces the war was no less crucial, but of a different order. Diplomacy, discretion, instinct, patience and a highly-developed critical intelligence were required, along with bravery and resourcefulness. An American military officer is success-oriented. "Can Do!" "Airborne All The Way!" "Above The Rest!" "The Difficult We Do Today, The Impossible Takes A Little

Longer!" are not idle slogans. The American officer is expected to produce, and if he does not the system grinds out someone who does. A thirty-four-year-old major is put down in a Vietnamese district and is expected to produce some progress. He must advise his counterparts, and whittle away at the Viet Cong "infrastructure," and see that the ARVN's and the civil defense forces have what they need. His men accompany patrols, and try to apply what they have learned at Leavenworth or Bragg or Benning. And when the reports go into MACV headquarters in Saigon at the end of each month, it is well that they represent some advance over the previous month. It is not for nothing that the reports are called "progress reports." They are exceedingly important; from them, among other sources, MACV assembles its estimate of the situation in South Vietnam: whether the allies are doing well or badly, the condition of enemy morale, the percentage of the country under the control of the Saigon government. From the estimate of the situation flows the military policy: will there be a multi-division operation in Tay Ninh province? What is the combat effectiveness of the 25th ARVN Division? How many Viet Cong inhabit Dinh Tuong province?

But the American adviser in Binh Chanh district south of Saigon, or at the 25th ARVN Division headquarters in Hau Nghia province, is in Vietnam for twelve months only. He does not see the war as a continuum. He sees it from January to January, or June to June, and frequently through the eyes of his Vietnamese counterpart, the man whom he is supposed to advise. That counterpart, the district chief or province chief, or division commander, has an equal interest in seeing progress made. His superiors in Vietnam have not placed *him* in Saigon to preside over a deteriorating military and political position. He is instructed to take as few casualties as possible, and there are invariably certain political considerations: to guard the rubber harvest in one province, to see that the rice gets to market (or, occasionally, that it doesn't get to market) in another. The American adviser, who does not speak the language, must depend on the pidgin English of his counterpart, or the word of his interpreter. Many advisers could plainly see that all was not well, but found it difficult to back up their impressions and very difficult to effect change. To stress the problems (or, as military officials in Saigon persisted in calling it, "the negative") required unusual confidence: MACV in Saigon graded its men, among other things, on how well they got along with the Vietnamese. If the Vietnamese were reporting a satisfactory situation, a state of affairs appreciated by the ARVN general staff, it was well for the American adviser to go along. Those who did not go along, and the examples were everywhere to find, were abruptly transferred and at tour's end found themselves in a logistics billet in Flagstaff, Arizona. It didn't happen all the time, but it happened often enough for the implication to be clear.

There was another, more subtle, compulsion. It was that the ARVN had been trained by the American Army. Its officers (Air Vice Marshal Ky, for example) had been to American training camps in Texas and Georgia. Reflections on the ARVN were reflections on the Americans as well, particularly the Americans at MACV in Saigon. The Americans were as reluctant to criticize Vietnamese military officials as an American football coach is reluctant to criticize his team.

Major General Fred C. Weyand, one of the senior Americans in Vietnam, once said that the principal duty of an adviser was to get along with his counterpart. That was what Weyand said publicly; one understood that his private comments were something else, but to the men the keynote was optimism. So there was harmony, and progress was reported. Eventually the reports reached Washington, where there was no reluctance to believe good news.

Not that these matters were ever easy. Two young American diplomats, one attached to the embassy in Saigon and the other to the White House in Washington, and both widely experienced in

Vietnam, once gave an informal lecture on the situation in Binh Chanh, the district that lay just south of Saigon on the fringes of the Mekong Delta. They had spent a week in Binh Chanh talking with Vietnamese and trying to gain, as one of them said, a feel for the situation. A suburb of the capital, Binh Chanh was thoroughly Viet Cong in outlook and political control; company-sized enemy units roamed its coconut groves at will, and intelligence from the population was fractional. The two Americans traced the roots of the revolutionary movement in the district (a movement which went back two decades), and then went on to talk a little of the personalities, loyalties and connections of the Viet Cong leaders. They discussed the government situation, the ability of the district chief and the quality of the various government forces in the area. There were ARVN battalions, three different ranks of civil defense forces, national police, and clandestine counter-terror teams. They sketched a history of the efforts at land reform, and the record of the several attempts at pacification, the so-called *hop tac* scheme which was an attempt to bring the Saigon suburbs under Saigon control. *Hop tac*, in yet a new form, was still ongoing; Binh Chanh was a priority area for pacification, and was so indicated on all the relevant project maps. The report of the two Americans was a pessimistic one, but what was impressive was the wealth of detail they had accumulated. Each detail, such as the names of the friends and relations of the Viet Cong district chief, made the tapestry a little richer and somehow more human—and also a good deal more complicated—but none of it brought Binh Chanh closer to solution. The two admitted that there were precious few answers to the question of how to pacify Binh Chanh district. One of them thought frankly that it could not be done at all.

Binh Chanh was one of more than 200 districts in South Vietnam. Experienced officials made the point that solutions to the problem could not really begin until the nature of Viet Cong control was understood. But the better it was understood, the more intractable it became. Ignorance in Vietnam was bliss. Nothing in an American military officer's background equipped him to deal with a situation of the complexity of the Binh Chanhs of South Vietnam. The problem, as reflective Americans were beginning to discover, was not primarily military. It was primarily political, just as the cliché had always said.

"EVERY quantitative measurement we have shows we are winning the war," said the Secretary of Defense, Robert McNamara. That was in 1962, when official preoccupations were elsewhere, and surely the Secretary could say the same today. All the indicators are good: enemy killed, weapons captured, *chieu hoi* (defectors) returned, encouraging reports of illness and disaffection from prisoners. "The enemy has failed in achieving his objectives while we have succeeded in achieving our objectives," General Westmoreland said in July, 1967. A million artillery shells are fired every month in the South. There are 175 sorties a day over the North. The equivalent of nine American combat divisions (in mid-1967) sweep the rice fields and forests. There are 2,000 helicopters, squadrons of PT boats in the Delta, and aircraft carriers and cruisers of the U.S. Navy in the South China Sea. The enemy has no sanctuary in South Vietnam: wherever he goes, the American infantry can follow—when the American infantry knows where he is. Increasingly sophisticated devices seek out heat at night, detect truck engines, smell body odors, listen for movement. The death toll rises. All the indicators point to improvement, progress, victory. Yet victory does not come. It seems as far away now as it ever did. Was it possible that the "quantitative measurements we have" do not apply to Vietnam? The likelihood of this may have occurred to General Maxwell D. Taylor and the chief of the U.S. Intelligence Board,

Clark Clifford, when the two returned from a tour of Vietnam and the Asian countries committed to her defense in August, 1967. Taylor declared that perhaps the war was misnamed, that it truly was "a Southeast Asian war." Perhaps, but it seemed the remark of a man who overturns the chessboard when his king is checked. The problem of progress in South Vietnam was not a matter of definitions of the war.

What was wanted was a new math, more likely a new calculus, to measure change and increments of change, to measure progress or the lack of it in a war without front lines. The proof is in the McNamara statement in 1962. He was logically right, and right again in 1965 when he said that the American troop withdrawal could begin in 1966. All the measurements pointed that way. And all the measurements were irrelevant. At least part of the reason was insufficient attention devoted to the Vietnamese, whose country it was and whose participation was crucial to the effort. Ton That Thien, a Catholic intellectual in Saigon who publishes in foreign magazines the views he feels unable to express in his own country, spoke of an alienated population:

> If the policies of the United States and the government of General Ky had popular support, it would be evident to all. The people of this country would raise the money and pay the taxes to support the war. The young men of the country would do the fighting against the enemy. The peasants in the countryside would not help the Viet Cong and would supply the intelligence needed to eliminate them. But we in Vietnam are doing none of these things. You are paying for this war . . . not the Vietnamese. You are fighting this war with American troops because the Vietnamese soldiers will not fight. The peasants are helping the Viet Cong and they are not giving you the intelligence you want. You are confronted with a society that opposes the present policies in the only way it can—with passive resistance.

Members of the civilian mission over the years have tried to construct new yardsticks, and the result has been an argument of almost Jesuitical complexity. The ablest American officials in South Vietnam have spent grueling hours around tables trying to figure out when a hamlet is pacified. The Vietnamese government assembles an eleven-point criteria that meets every test that can be devised, from the elimination of hatred to the eradication of disease. There are six-point criteria and three-point criteria, the simple statements of the blunt and hard-minded ("the place is pacified when I don't get shot at going through it") to the almost mystical formulations of the scholars of the Vietnamese *Weltan-schauung* ("Vietnam will be pacified when the villagers decide it is pacified and they will decide on the basis of the ear of heaven"). But there are still no criteria that can be applied by the American government and simply stated by the President of the United States. What is the quantitative measurement of passive resistance?

It came back finally to Binh Chanh district, and the unmistakable implication of the findings of the two Americans: that the people of the district preferred the Viet Cong to the Saigon government. As the bombings increased and civilian casualties mounted, more Vietnamese would put their skins before their hearts and minds; they would become neutral, and hope for an end to the war. But their sentiments were not with the Saigon government, or with the Americans.

THE AMERICAN public perception of the war in Vietnam is different from that of other wars in part because the scholars and academics have been able to examine it. The war ends up reviewed, as an off-Broadway play is reviewed in its performances and themes, careful attention particularly paid to themes—"roles," as they were called in Vietnam. It is the first war where an academic could walk about undisturbed (and relatively safe) and probe and take soundings. They were linguists and anthropologists, historians and political scientists, and the best of them, men like Bernard Fall, Gerald Hickey and Paul Mus, brought perceptions to Vietnam that were unavailable in other wars. Often financed by research grants from the Department of Defense, teams of psychologists, sociologists and economists roamed the land, interviewing peasants and colonels and writing reports and dissertations all aimed at finding out *what was going on.* There were reports on the role of women, on the role of the Regional and Popular Forces, on the *chieu hoi,* on government propaganda, on enemy "weapons systems," on the behavior of the ARVN. It is said that one of the finest reports ever produced about the Americans in Vietnam was RAMJET—Roles and Missions Joint Evaluation Team, written by a group of men inside the embassy. All of these reports, like the celebrated Sloat report on the attitudes of four Vietnamese to the American presence, in one way or another got into the mainstream of opinion on Vietnam; though they are classified reports, the men who put them together like to talk. Not surprisingly, many of the ablest scholars and academics had grave doubts about the war itself. These doubts crept into the studies, or rather informed the frames of reference around which the studies were built. The military critics of the plethora of studies complained that the civilians were interested only in the things that went wrong. And of course the military critics were right. *Schadenfreude.*

The best, and always the wittiest, reports were written by the scholars and academics. The passage that follows was written by an economist, and represents his recommendation for a revised pacification program. It was a memorandum designed to influence the policy-makers in the American Embassy and in Washington, although it is doubtful that it did so. I have left the jargon unexplained, since that is part of its charm:

In brief, the new approach may be summarized: clear the contested areas, pacify the "blue" areas. Clear with military/police effort, "pacify" with cadre and other civil efforts; not in the same spot, but the one within the other, which is the true meaning of the "oilspot" approach. If the formula above sounds familiar, it must be emphasized that it implies an approach in sharp contrast to the current 1967 RD plan. A year's efforts along the lines suggested—in the four-fold aspects: (a) military clearing in contested areas, (b) RD efforts in "blue" areas, (c) the development of cadre, plans and RVNAF, and (d) national-level political evolution toward representative, nationalistic government—could see by the year's end a considerably greater increase in the cleared areas than the 1967 plan is likely to permit plus the actual generation, unlikely otherwise, of significant public support and participation in a number of relatively secure areas. From that base, and with a better prepared RVNAF, cadre, and plans, it would be realistic to aim at greater expansion both of the "cleared" and the "pacified" areas in the subsequent six months: which would take us, as it happens, into the fall of 1968 . . .

In an attempt to bring his own methodology to bear on the war in Vietnam, Secretary McNamara has dispatched bright and audacious young men to Saigon to construct yardsticks for him that have more relevance than body counts and kill ratios and expressions of optimism. The men brought back a number of new formulas, one of which was the CERR—or Contact Effectiveness Response Ratio. It sought to establish a formula to measure the effectiveness of the various branches of the Vietnamese armed forces when they came to do battle with the Viet Cong. The CERR showed, among other things, that the underpaid, underfed, underarmed, undermanned, and generally neglected Regional and Popular Forces were at least twice as effective as the relatively pampered regular battalions of the ARVN. In one divisional area of operations, the four-province sector of the 25th ARVN Division, the RF and PF squads were found to be approximately four times as effective as the entire 12,000-man division. Other studies, conducted strictly on the basis of cost and effectiveness, confirmed the CERR. Thus, mathematicians joined the consensus of opinion of men long in the field: much of the ARVN was not pulling its weight. But the important point was that nothing was done about the 25th ARVN Division. In fact its commander, General Chinh, remained; the American adviser, Colonel Cecil Honeycutt, the man who knew what was happening and blew the whistle, was sent home.

In time, Secretary McNamara would consider staffing MACV with some of his bright civilian analysts, and running it like a little Pentagon. The colonels would do the fighting and the civilians would analyze, and make the estimates. But it didn't happen. The bright young civilians were not popular with the colonels, and vice versa.

THE REGULAR members of the civilian mission were with the war year in and year out, some of them up to three years and more. It was not a lifetime commitment, or even an extended one. A man came to Vietnam on a tour of duty, not for the duration. The principal reason for this seemed to me to be the psychological imbalance in the American approach to the war: there was no call-up, the reserves were not mobilized, and there was no economic dislocation at home. Perhaps more important, as Walter Lippmann has pointed out, none of the senior, or even junior, members of the Johnson Administration has resigned in order to take up arms in Vietnam. There was no crisis atmosphere anywhere in America, and somehow this fact was perfectly clear in the most remote base camp or USAID program office in Vietnam. Why should a man leave his wife and family for "the duration" (military officials spoke equably of a twenty years' war) when the rest of America was conducting business as usual, and colleagues were practicing classical diplomacy as political officers in the embassy in Rome. Saigon was itself a microcosm of this, with cocktail parties and miniskirts on the one hand

and the bombing of billets on the other. The schizophrenia translated into impermanence: high officials worried along with the Saigon government that Washington was prepared to liquidate its position in Vietnam, and they saw that event not in global or Southeast Asian terms but in Vietnamese terms, which meant personal terms. There were marriage troubles everywhere, and the uneasiness about the war itself made it difficult for a man to justify an indefinite separation from his wife and family. There was no sense of being with the war to its conclusion, and whether that contributed to the inability of anyone to see the end, or vice versa, is impossible to say. Perhaps both. But it was a part of the psychology.

When the civilians gave way, it was usually to despair and disillusion, the wartime equivalent to a character in a Somerset Maugham short story. Some endured, working quietly and efficiently and living in Saigon villas as though they were in Algiers or Georgetown. It was possible to live that way, with imported wine and an automobile, tennis at the *Cercle Sportif* and an occasional Vietnamese lady. Those who did were about the only American civilians who remained themselves, detached from the tumult. They were also the ones who seemed to enjoy Vietnam and the Vietnamese, in a relationship other than that of the mongoose and the cobra or the parent and the child. They reacted to Vietnam exactly as Vietnam reacted to them, with detachment, suspicion, politesse and humor. The sheer effort put into the job was enormous, and the pride in long hours unraveling the impossibly twisted threads of Vietnam justified. The long hours, particularly for civilians in the field, sometimes had the reverse effect. The men became unraveled, a condition which often resulted in startling fantasies. One of the most common was the taking of a Vietnamese lady "for keeps." It did not happen often, but frequently enough to become a source of concern to officials whose business it was to worry about that sort of thing. It was as if the Vietnamese problem had become so intractable, the Vietnamese themselves so opaque, that the only solution was individual and personal. I suppose it was like the copulatory theory of American race relations: that all will not be well until there is complete and unselfconscious intermarriage.

But the men who were successful kept it all at arm's length, served their tours (usually more than one), listened and learned and left the country wiser and older, but not fundamentally marked by the experience. These were the ones who came to Vietnam unmarried and unattached. As the civilian mission grew, it attracted more and more men who were, for one reason or another, in flight. Some fled from boredom, some from problems of money or family or health; most from women. Sex explained a good deal about the attitudes of Americans in Vietnam: part of it was the country itself and the war, but most of it was what the men brought to the war. The absence of wives in the Saigon atmosphere was one of the most unfortunate facts of the American presence. It was not helpful.

Of course there were exceptions, many of them, to the generalizations above. There was, for example, no explanation at all for the young official in the field—unmarried, to all appearances a stable man—who announced his intention to marry a fifty-year-old Vietnamese woman who had made her living as a prostitute. He said he was in love with her. And what could be made of the young officer in the field who was asked to give a briefing to his superiors in Saigon? Summoned to the embassy, he stood and said: "I was out on the road . . . I was out on the road . . . out on the road . . . the road." He had been in Vietnam one year.

Nearly all the American civilians felt that if America endured, victory, for what it was worth, would eventually come. Negotiations were rarely mentioned, for no information on them was available in Saigon. That was a Washington syndrome, and somehow irrelevant to the men who were dealing with main-force battalions, cadre teams, aid programs or the Viet Cong political apparatus. Very few civilians who were in Vietnam for more than a year could argue convincingly in support of the American presence; not that the question was very often asked. In fact in eighteen months in South Vietnam I do not recall a single serious conversation on the matter. It was never a question of the implications for Southeast Asia, but the implications for the Americans and the Vietnamese. Americans were broadly agreed that the commitments to the Vietnamese who chose to fight precluded any abrupt withdrawal; to do so would be to consign them to the ash-heap of history, and a Viet Cong death sentence as well. It was felt that American honor could not countenance this. But most civilians, if they had a choice to write the original Eisenhower letter or not to write it, which is to say to become involved with the fate of Vietnam or not to become involved, would have chosen not to. The most idealistic, and therefore most appealing, Americans in the country felt the need for a social revolution very deeply, almost as an expiation of American guilt for changing the tone and temper of the war, and prolonging it. We had gone so far, we must now make the future attractive for those who survive. These feelings were complicated by the increasingly heavy totals of American casualties, and the complaints of Vietnamese indifference grew as the casualty list grew. The argument was an emotional one, but Saigon was an emotional place: quite simply it was that the 12,000 dead Americans should not have died in vain. For nothing. For an army and a people who themselves had no stomach for the struggle. For a social order long since extinct. It was no good arguing that bringing the boys home would save lives, that it was pointless adding dead to dead. The point was that too many had already died, and those lives had somehow to be given meaning.

There was no affection for the Viet Cong, and Ho Chi Minh's regime in the North was regarded as barbarous. If there had to be an occupation of South Vietnam, most Americans concluded that the South Vietnamese were better off in Washington's hands than

Hanoi's. On these points, there was broad agreement. What was in dispute was what would have been the course of events had not the United States intervened; that, and of course the policy itself.

There were so many variations on the broad theme of American policy of prosecuting the war in Vietnam that to reproduce them would be to assemble a shopping list of every article, book, monograph, speech, statement and banner of the last ten years. The two broad streams of dissent in Vietnam, which had little to do with whether or not the Americans should be there (we *were* in Vietnam, and that was that), swirled around the conception of the war. Was it a war which could be won by force of arms, or was it a political war? It was, of course, both. So which conception was to dominate? The generals said it was a war first and a social revolution second, and the diplomats said the reverse. Often they said nothing. Could the Americans win it, or was it still primarily a war for the Vietnamese to win? It was, of course, both. But, as with the first argument, the generals eventually won—or events made it inevitable, given the capacities of the Vietnamese, that if the Americans were to stay in Vietnam it would perforce become an American war. The Vietnamese became outsiders looking in, and as they looked in, like Scott Fitzgerald's poor kids, their noses pressed against the windows of the country club, they became envious, then resentful, and finally they withdrew. It was easier advising Americans than advising Vietnamese, so the attention of MACV shifted. As American casualties grew, Westmoreland would become increasingly concerned with the American part of the war, which is to say the large-unit war against the battalions of the North. In May, 1967, Westmoreland took control of the pacification program as well. It was decided that to pacify meant to bring military security to the village; you had to have security, the colonels explained, before you could have social justice, the *sine qua non* of winning the allegiance of the people to the Saigon government. It was a military matter, and therefore

75

properly an MACV affair. The civilians were left to analyze and interpret, and management passed to the colonels. About all the civilians had left was the advisory effort to the Vietnamese government. What remained of the civilian interest in Vietnam was an aid program, as in Turkey. It made the attitudes of the military, particularly the senior officers, even more important.

ONCE every two or three months General Westmoreland would summon the press corps regulars to his conference room at MACV for a progress report on the war. This would be the official version of the state of the war, and everyone made an effort to attend. These sessions had a startling similarity, which I have realized only after consulting my notes on the half dozen or so that I attended. The general gave the order of battle, ours and theirs, and then went on to a discussion of strategy and tactics. It was not a discussion of Vietnamese strategy and tactics, but American strategy and tactics; sometimes Westmoreland would refer to the Free World Forces, sometimes to the Allies. But he meant the Americans. There was always a monsoon offensive, either just beginning in the highlands or just ending in the North (or the reverse), an enemy effort to "cut the country in half" (spoiled by American offensive maneuvers), an estimate of two or three enemy divisions in, over or under the Demilitarized Zone, an improvement in the security around Saigon, equilibrium in the Delta. Captured documents showed the enemy was hurting. The Americans were on the offensive, the North Vietnamese and the Viet Cong were on the defensive. But there was no sign of a break. Are there any questions?

Haltingly and diffidently a correspondent would observe that the pattern did not seem much changed from the last time the general had met with the press. Westmoreland would pull himself to his full height of six feet one inch, pat the blouse of his immaculately starched fatigues, gaze at the correspondent through clear blue eyes, imperceptibly raise and jut out his jaw, and rumble the statistics his colonels had assembled for the occasion: enemy KIA, weapons captured, rice seized, *chieu hoi* defectors, documents purporting to show a decline in enemy morale. Occasionally a document would admit failure of this or that objective and that, too, would be cited as evidence of success. The correspondent listened to the statistics, and never followed up the question. He would nod glumly and the general would ask if he had answered fully and frankly and the correspondent would say Yes, he had.

So he had. It was a great and winning performance, and contributed materially to the generally good relations between the correspondents and the senior officers at MACV. Westmoreland's relations with the Saigon press were excellent, and he was never caught in a gaffe. He never predicted when the war would end, nor would he forecast the end of the beginning or the beginning of the end, or when the corner would be turned or if, indeed, there was a corner. He would only say (accurately, by the statistics) that there was progress, and imply that the more men he had the more progress he would make. But he was very careful about that. At the end of the briefing, Westmoreland would leave the room first, the press corps rising as a mark of respect.

A four-star general is a king among princes, and if the four-star looks and behaves as Westmoreland looked and behaved, he is a king among kings. He is not a man with whom to argue or trifle. Barry Zorthian, the USIS director in Saigon, was greatly amused at the feckless performance of the American press when dealing with Westmoreland. Zorthian contended that the press alternately protected and pampered the general, persistently refusing to tax him with embarrassing questions. He regarded the general as the foremost practitioner of the art of public relations in Saigon: Zorthian insisted that sophisticated correspondents laughed in his face when he gave precisely the same answers, with precisely the same statistics, that were received gravely and seriously when they came from Westmoreland. Of course Zorthian was right. General Westmoreland was protected (if that is the word) precisely for the reason that he was unable to dissemble; he was so transparently honest and dedicated that no one thought of holding him accountable for the ambiguities and curiosities of American policy. It was all right to ask a colonel why the ARVN refused to fight, but somehow the same question asked of Westmoreland was phrased delicately and with circumlocutions:

Do you think, Sir, that the performance of ARVN has improved. Answer: Definitely.

The same question, asked informally of a colonel, was put this way:

The ARVN 25th Division has killed only four Viet Cong since last Thanksgiving. The division commander is both corrupt and a coward. Why is he not relieved?

Westmoreland was admired, both as a man and as a general, and my suspicion is that the press knew that he would have to dodge the question on the theory that no useful purpose could be served by candor. He had enough troubles with the Vietnamese without adding to them by indiscretions in the press. It was a curious fact that however much critics, newspapermen and others, thought that Vietnam strategy was misguided or wrong, Westmoreland never took the blame for it. Neither did Henry Cabot Lodge. The fault was found either at staff or at province, or most often in Washington. Administration critics inside the embassy were dumbfounded that the ambassador and the general were never called to account. I have never read a searching analysis of the Vietnam performance of either Westmoreland or Lodge, and I never expect to. It is not somehow writable, not now—and probably not even when all the returns are in. Until the future can be seen clearly it is impossible to know whether the strategy inside the country (one specifically exempts the bombing of the North) was right or wrong. But even if that can be seen with any certainty, will it be possible to name the authors of the strategy? Were both the ambassador and the general prisoners of events?

Was not everyone a prisoner of events, caught in a quagmire, watching the falling dominoes of increased commitment: money became aircraft, which in turn necessitated advisers who became battalions, then brigades, then divisions, then corps, until finally there were 500,000 men in the country with no one able to say how or why it happened? Inside the madhouse there was a logic, and the more time you spent in the field looking at dead men the more powerful the logic. And every time you talked to a general you were told that things were going very well—a reversal here and there, but generally going very well. They saw the valor, and from the valor victory.

One of the last great distinctions among men is between generals and everybody else. It is not a matter of money, for a full general's salary is still under $25,000 a year. There are certain perquisites, but these are insignificant compared to the expense accounts of successful corporation executives, to name the obvious parallel. Most of it has to do with command. Generals do not lead, they command; subordinates do not follow, they obey. Obedience is an unfamiliar word in the vocabulary of the 1960's, almost an anachronism in liberated America.

The typical general is white, Anglo-Saxon, Protestant, mid-fifties, mid-western. Surprisingly, many are from the South, the only American region to retain a military tradition in families. His roots are middle-class; his politics, if any, conservative. His loyalties are no more complicated than most Americans with a similar background, save one important difference: a strong and emotional tie to the armed forces, and specifically to the unit to which he is attached (or commands). A lieutenant commands a platoon, a captain a company, a lieutenant colonel a battalion, a colonel a regiment or integrated brigade, a brigadier general an independent brigade, a major general a division, a lieutenant general a corps, and a full general an entire army. At any of these ranks, a man may be on another man's staff—but the objective is to secure one's own command. The distinction begins with the independent brigade. All military officers are subject to orders from above, but some are less subject than others. General officers, beginning with brigadiers, command independent units . . . which fight . . . other men.

There is no greater responsibility than a general's, and around it hovers a kind of mystique. There are a whole set of assumptions that go with being a general which are absent from politics, business, medicine and corporate law. The first of these is that the general has gone through combat and is personally brave. Another is that he is smart enough and adroit enough to leave his fellows behind at that crucial point when a major is promoted to lieutenant colonel and, later, when the lieutenant colonel is promoted to full colonel. If there is a snag in the career chain, the wise officer opts out, and thus the second difference between the military profession and the others. The bright lawyer or motor company vice president, dissatisfied with company policies, resigns and goes to work for the opposition. In the American military, there is no opposition. Sam Rayburn, the late Speaker of the House of Representatives, had a maxim for incoming congressmen: . . . To get along, go along. . . . It is equally true for military services. Initiative can propel a man from captain to major, and sometimes from major to lieutenant colonel. But at that point caution commends itself. In the American military services, expressions of conventional wisdom are raised to the level of an art form.

The military staff system, short on initiative and long on efficiency, was devised for the management of a conventional war, where too much individual initiative was self-destructive. There, it was a matter of making certain that orders were executed fully and promptly with no slip-up, in a coordinated attack which might involve 40,000 men. In Vietnam, strategy and tactics were often improvised—with general officers sometimes overseeing (literally, from a helicopter 1,500 feet above the battle) the operations of a battalion or one or two companies. But even with the improvisations, many of the officers seemed rigid and found it difficult to break the traditional molds of conventional warfare.

They were some of the most attractive men in Vietnam, from the old-shoe, rumpled, unshaven manner of Major General William R. Peers (commander of the 4th Infantry Division, and a practiced guerrilla fighter from World War II days in Burma) to Central Casting's spit-and-polish image of a modern major general, Jack Norton (commander of the 1st Cavalry Division, Airmobile). Westmoreland's father had been a small-town businessman, Norton's a colonel, and the father of the dour, aggressive and feisty commander of the 1st Infantry Division, Major General William DePuy, a banker in North Dakota. There was an open-shirted masculinity about dinner in a general's tent in An Khe that made it somehow preferable to the mixed tables in Saigon. Norton's general's mess had a white cloth on the table and polite waiters passed large, dry Martinis; there was cameraderie and storytelling, and Norton would always ask his guests to make short speeches. They were heckled, and one was reminded of a fraternity at college; except these were men who were fighting a war.

The generals talked of military tactics in their off-hours in precisely the manner of dedicated insurance executives arguing about premiums. But unlike the insurance man, the military man is ill-at-ease with outsiders, which is to say civilians. His attitude is either defensive or condescending, as if he had a special wisdom withheld from civilians; but all of it somehow understandable within the context of "the military." The perfect battle does not exist, and post-mortems invariably reveal egregious errors. The wise journalist may laugh about his cloudy crystal ball, for he knows that nothing is written on stone tablets and no permanent harm done. But when a military operation is fouled, men die. When the logistics supply line clogs, it costs the taxpayer millions. It is difficult for the military man to point out that error is inherent in any battle: they can say it among themselves, but not to outsiders. Such an admission requires a sense of irony and fatalism, and it is precisely these characteristics which are bred out of successful generals.

IF YOU were in Vietnam for eighteen months you were an old-timer, a veteran analyst and a man who knew where the bodies were buried. You were entitled to respect. If the months had done no more than produce a kind of mind-wearying monotony where every statement pro or con produced a "Yes, but" answer, you were entitled to even more respect—except from the men who came in and out of the country on temporary assignments, declaring that none of the regulars (either diplomats or journalists) were seeing the forest for the trees. Of course it was true, and so was the reverse. There was one American official who had been in the country since the early 1950's. Strangely, no one was certain precisely what he did; but he was said to be happy in South Vietnam, and satisfied that progress was being made.

Progress was always being made. Progress was the most important product in Vietnam. It could be found anywhere, in the unlikeliest circumstances. Once in early 1967 Robert Shaplen of *The New Yorker* arrived at Tan Son Nhut Airport in Saigon and was kept waiting for nearly an hour while his passport was shuffled back and forth among immigration officials. The passport was a new one, and Shaplen had neglected to secure a visa. Not that a visa was ordinarily required for entry; Shaplen had made dozens of trips in and out of Saigon, with and without visas, and had always breezed through airport formalities. Now, watching the little man behind the desk meticulously fiddling with the thick pages, Shaplen became angry, finally enraged, and in blunt Anglo-Saxon demanded that the officials get on with it so he could leave for downtown Saigon. One of them told him to be quiet and sit down and then, almost as an afterthought, flung a folding chair at him. It was an unparalleled act for the normally polite Vietnamese, and Shaplen was telling the story one night to an embassy official. The official was impressed, because it indicated to him that the Vietnamese bureaucracy was working. "Hell, Bob," the official said. "It shows they're really taking hold at the airport."

Equally, progress was never made. It always foundered in a swamp of incriminating detail. Listening to Americans discuss the rural reconstruction/revolutionary development/pacification program (whichever name was current, and convenient) with its eleven-point *ap doi moi* or six-point *ap tan sinh,* its jargon and its rhetorical embellishments was a rare delight. It was best and funniest when an old-timer confronted a newcomer. The new man had typically received some sort of orientation course, including a go at the language, but it took some time to digest the ideas that went with the words. It was not an easy matter for an inexperienced man to confidently discuss the eleven-point *ap doi moi,* let alone *hop tac,* as casually as the importance of SEATO or the logistics requirements of a company of infantry.

The old-timer had heard it all before, and had warned his companion against being taken in by anything. Don't believe everything you're told, he'd say; but he meant, don't believe *anything* you're told. It was a confusing country, with countless pitfalls. Watch for the lie. No one in Vietnam really knew when he was lying or telling the truth, but some of them knew. Watch for the ones who *know that they're lying.* They've been lying for years. It's up to us to find them out.

"We were in Long An today," the new man said, naming the province that lay south of Saigon at the top of the Delta. He had gone with an expert from the embassy to look into the behavior of one of the 59-man revolutionary development cadre teams.

"Ummmm," said the old-timer. "I suppose you talked to Wilson."

"Yes," the new man said. "An excellent briefing. Really first-class. Of course, we got out to see for ourselves."

"Ummm," said the old-timer.

"The cadre is working, I'll say that," the new man went on. "But the chief isn't sleeping in the hamlet, and neither is the cadre, and I should judge that not more than four of the eleven points are being met."

"Did you go alone to the hamlet, or with a Vietnamese?"

"Why, we went with a Vietnamese," the new man said.

"Which one?" the old-timer asked urgently.

"Why, the district chief."

"Ah," said the old-timer. "Perhaps that's why the cadre seemed to be working."

"The district chief told me that the Viet Cong infrastructure was being rooted out and the government rooted in. He said that the aspirations of the people were being fulfilled, thanks to the Americans and the new budget which permitted the fence to be built."

"Well, it was all laid on, you see," the old-timer said. "The district chief laid it on, told the cadre to be working when you arrived. I'm surprised Sam Wilson permitted a visit so obviously laid on like that. It doesn't mean anything. It's meaningless."

"It looked pretty good to me," the other said.

"Interesting fellow, that district chief," said the old-timer, calmly. "Viet Minh background, they say. Corrupt and lazy of course, and there are rumors that he is VC. Brother lives in Hanoi, cousin works for CAS in Ban Me Thuot. Sister lives in Paris with his mother, who has the license to import grapefruit juice at Danang. The mother used to be the mistress of General Nguyen, who now lives in Bangkok. He is supposed to take money from the *deuxième bureau,* and then of course there were suspicions about the rice crop. But he seems to run a tight shop although his English is faulty. I have never been certain he knew what we were saying to him, or what he was saying to us. But not at all the worst district chief in the province, although it wouldn't be well to believe all he says."

"Oh," said the newcomer.

"He's typical of Long An," the older man said, now grown expansive. "You must remember the experience of Long An"—here he went to his blackboard and flipped down a series of charts, bisected by lines and marked by little flags of different colors—"agrovilles, strategic hamlets, new life hamlets, the *ap dinh sinh,* the *ap doi moi,* the Ruff-Puff, the cadre and all the rest. We've tried to iron out some of the problems with census grievance but, culturally speaking, you know the capacities of the RevDev ministry. Thang has his worries with Ty, and of course there's old Ace to worry about and *his* people. The PRU's have been cutting off heads again and we still don't know the aspirations of the people, although Lord knows we've tried." The old-timer went on to mention all the pacification schemes of *hop tac.*

"Well," said the young man, who had understood about one-fourth of what the old-timer had said. "The district chief seemed quite hopeful of progress. He mentioned a bridge . . . "

"Of course he did," the old-timer soothed, "of course he did."

WHAT the Americans desperately needed was some area of Vietnamese expertise, something done well and seen to be done well, that could be pointed to with pride and displayed to visiting congressmen and journalists—perhaps more than that, to give the Americans themselves a sense that something was happening, that progress was being made and that the Vietnamese were assuming responsibility. The word was nation-building.

The Vietnamese themselves are the best commentators on the difficulty of nation-building. One of the most acerbic is the Catholic intellectual Ton That Thien, a complicated figure, half-reactionary and half-revolutionary and all nationalist, a press secretary to Ngo Dinh Diem, and most recently managing editor of a Saigon newspaper banned by the government. Thien gave this account of the progress, or lack of it, of the Vietnamese civil service:

> . . . France started training a new elite to induce the Vietnamese to serve. The French colonial administration offered them special privileges, including a generous, or rather overgenerous, grant of land—part of which was seized from the peasants—and a status close to that of the French nationals. Some of the holdings were so large that they were referred to in popular parlance as "land over which the stork can fly endlessly without encountering obstacles" (ruong co bay thang canh). It was from this source that the new class derived its immense wealth. This inevitably alienated it from the rural population, partly because of the income gap separating the one from the other, partly because the rural inhabitants looked upon the new class as despoilers. Moreover the new elite acquired new ways which made them feel closer to the French than to their compatriots, and this further widened the gulf between them and the peasants.*

The alienation of the "new class" of civil servants, Thien went on, meant that social stability was preserved outwardly, but in fact

---

* Ton That Thien, Vietnam: *A Case of Social Alienation*, International Affairs Review.

was being inexorably eroded because it was plain where the real power lay. "No important position could be attained by a Vietnamese official, without the approval of the French colonial government," Thien wrote. "It was from the cities that the new officials were recruited. To qualify for high government positions, new diplomas were required, and these could be gained only through a long and expensive period of schooling obtainable only in the cities. The peasants were therefore excluded from the high, as well as the middle, positions." What had happened was a systematic separation of the peasantry from the government. The new system, instituted by the French, was aimed principally (and logically enough) at the preservation of colonial interests.

Ton That Thien's view was that the Americans were perpetuating this system, and making it inevitable that the Viet Cong would keep control of the revolutionary atmosphere. The two most important social, or political, ideals to the Vietnamese are nationalism and sovereignty. Both were the property of the Communists, as the Vietnamese bureaucracy worked increasingly in the service of the Americans. It was never put quite as crassly as that, but that is what it amounted to. The ministries in Saigon became agencies for the execution of American programs.

Seen from Washington and the American Embassy in Saigon, the Vietnamese effort always seemed to be several paces behind. The more the Americans prodded it, the more it lagged. The aid budget was so large, something on the order of $400,000,000 a year when everything was considered, that it could not be administered effectively. A school was built, but there were no books or teachers. Books were imported, and then sent to a village where there were no schools (or, as happened in one village, were consigned to a teacher who was told that she would be responsible for them; she forthwith locked them in a cabinet and told the children they were to be looked at, not read). Funds were made available for a bridge, and the bridge was never built but somehow the funds were spent. The confusion was made worse by the Vietnamese habit of automatic agreement to almost any proposal (as long as it did not seriously alter the status quo), and of laughter at odd times and places. The Vietnamese laugh both from amusement and embarrassment and you can never tell which it is. The twenty years' war was occasion for both. Being fundamentally polite, and anxious to please, they were happy to affix signatures to documents authorizing projects which they never intended (as the Americans liked to say) implementing. There would be a suitable discussion period, in the rabbit-warren offices of USAID or the vast airy structures housing the Ministry of Education or the Ministry of Finance, and then there would be a sign-off. Washington, which set unusual store by documents signed and sealed, assumed that when the Vietnamese agreed to something, the thing would be done. Often the objective was to get the piece of paper from one desk to another. To the Vietnamese, it usually meant getting rid of a persistent American official; to the Americans, it meant a checkmark, a tick—*Done!*—beside a long outstanding project. Washington assumed that because there was a civil service, and French-trained at that, it worked. Embassy officials who dealt with Vietnamese knew better: that it was a civil service competent to perform certain rituals, like marriage licenses, death certificates, and (*in extremis*) automobile registrations, but very little else. Its members were grossly underpaid, badly dealt with, and usually had to take second jobs to make ends meet. It was a long way from the Mandarinate of the old French days.

Of course there were bribes. These often took the form of trips to America. The Americans assumed that once the Vietnamese saw how the future worked, they would take to it and bring its logic back to Vietnam. Thus there were delegations of labor leaders sent to Detroit, farmers sent to New Jersey, journalists sent to Seattle and New York, lady business executives enrolled for a short course at the Harvard Business School in Cambridge, Massachusetts. These groups were usually accompanied by an interpreter, who would translate the future into Vietnamese. Hardheaded Americans in Saigon contended that all these trips did was remove many of the most responsible (if not the ablest) Vietnamese officials from the scene at the time they were most needed, *i.e.,* now, when the war was being fought. Thus, the province chief of Quang Nam, Nguyen Huu Chi, a graceful and languid product of Michigan State University, undertook a six-week lecture tour of America at the time the Buddhist militants occupied his capital city; the foreign editor of *Chinh Luan,* the most influential newspaper in Saigon, arrived in New York in April, 1967, and coincidentally was able to witness the massive demonstration against the war in Vietnam. The editor, Vu Thuy Hoang, returned to Saigon baffled by the enormity of the United States. "It's such an immense country," he said in wonder. And what of the demonstrations? "Ah," he said, "there was no violence. It was a peaceful demonstration." Then, "Were all those who marched Communists?"

Difficulties were compounded by the language barrier, which was really more moat than barrier. It was an odd fact that the Vietnamese appeared to learn English quicker and with greater fluency than the Americans learned Vietnamese. It required a six-month cram course for an American to grasp even the fundamentals of that six-tone language, and then unless there was constant practice, the trick would be lost. Few Americans took the trouble or were made to take the trouble to learn the language thoroughly, and the Vietnamese knew this and in candid moments would comment on it. The fact is that neither language could be successfully translated into the other—witness "the stork flying endlessly over the land without encountering obstacles." Vietnamese verbs do not change tense and the sense of time is therefore indefinite. The personal pronoun "I" does not exist in the abstract; discourse is undertaken in the third person ("a citizen" or "your cousin"—if the speaker is a cousin of the person to whom he is talking) and a man's identity, his sense of himself, is always in relation to something, or someone, else—usually something, or someone, having to do with the village, which is one reason the village is so important in Vietnamese life. The implications of this for the Vietnamese personality are vast and immensely complicated, and for the language itself equally so. What was translated, be it a conversation or an official document, was but an approximation of meaning, how proximate depending on the sensitivity of the translator. It was no accident, I thought, that the Americans who seemed most sympathetic to the Vietnamese were men whose origins were Middle Eastern: in one case an Armenian, in another a Lebanese, in a third a Greek. The intrigues, the convolutions, the complexities, the mysteries of cultures were not frustrating to these men; they thrived on them, particularly the intrigues.

The Americans who did learn the language (and there were perhaps two dozen with real fluency) understood the people, and their moods and enthusiasms, much better than those who did not. It was a treat to watch Vietnamese-speaking Americans. Their personalities changed as they spoke, and normally droll diplomats became smiling, bowing, laughing Orientals as they sang along with friends, pursing lips and shrugging, washing their hands and saying *Yaaa*. *Yaaa* was the staple word in Vietnamese, indicative of almost anything depending on the accent, and where it was placed. To the untrained ear the language seemed babel, repetitive and imprecise and full of rhetorical flourishes. *Hya yyya nyo fra tralee.*

Or *traloo*. The difficulty, if it can be called that, became greatest (not that it mattered much) when the Americans put English words to Vietnamese programs. Occasionally, or more than occasionally, the process was reversed and the Vietnamese were forced to translate American programs into Vietnamese. When the Americans wanted to change the name of a program, presumably to invest it with different emphasis and tone, the Vietnamese always readily agreed. It made no difference to them. The Vietnamese word stayed the same, whatever the Americans wanted to call it. Thus the efforts in the countryside evolved from strategic hamlets and new life hamlets to rural reconstruction and revolutionary development. With each new label there was to be a new, presumably more effective, program. But the Vietnamese word for these schemes remained, almost from the beginning, "construction." Prime Minister Ky once said that the phrase "revolutionary development" had no equivalent in Vietnamese; it would not translate at all. "It comes out meaningless," Ky said.*

"If a man speaks two languages he is two men," an old French-speaking Vietnamese official in the Delta told me, by way of explanation that the Americans in his country remained Americans and therefore alien and would never understand the Vietnamese until they learned the language. The session with the old man was delightful. He had learned a classical, elegant French but not English. He said he was too old now to learn English, just as he was too old to predict the course of the war. He said that language was the *sine*

---

* The Americans in Vietnam were always changing the lexicon, sometimes even the English and French words. In early 1967, a directive came to Saigon from Washington to cease to use the word "cadre" for the RD teams. Cadre, it was explained, was a Communist word and therefore offensive. The substitute was to be "worker." Equally, in 1966, the military stopped calling the North Vietnamese Army by the popular acronym PAVN (People's Army of North Vietnam, pronounced pavin). "It just adds to their propaganda, calling them a people's army," a colonel explained. "Our army is just as much a people's army as theirs is. We call our army ARVN." So the PAVN became the NVA (pronounced en-vee-ay).

qua non of cooperation, and until the Americans learned that lesson there would be two separate lives, American and Vietnamese, and the war would never be won, or ended, and progress never made. I said we would probably not know the importance of language until the war was over and all the memoirs written. The old man smiled at that.

4

THE EXILES

IT WAS IMPOSSIBLE to know what they were thinking. There were myriad studies and reports, and in the American mission "memcons" (memos of conversation) with this or that Vietnamese. These were meant to help explain to the authorities in Washington the Vietnamese view of events in South Vietnam. The memcons were never very satisfactory, either as literature or as information, and the usual response was, Isn't that *fascinating*. The Vietnamese, wisely from their point of view, were anxious that nothing definite appear on the record since the essence of political life in South Vietnam was the avoidance of taking a stand on anything. Elsewhere, in other world capitals more sophisticated in semantics, this was known as keeping all the options open. In my opinion the classic commentary on American-Vietnamese verbal exchanges was made by Prime Minister Ky, in an interview with R. W. Apple of the *New York Times*. It was just before the presidential election in September, 1967, and Apple was interested in learning what, if anything, Ambassador Ellsworth Bunker was saying to the prime minister on the question of illegal campaigning.

"Oh, I tell him that everything is perfectly honest and aboveboard and then he smiles," the prime minister said. "He tells me he believes me, and then I smile."

IN THESE conversations you were made to feel more than you understood. It was political haiku, flying blind most of the time and never more so than when it was necessary to deal with Vietnamese youth. Saigon had its middle-class teeny-boppers and hippies, and the impression was that youth was as alienated there as it was in San Francisco. The feeling was of a society deranged by war, with no indication where it was heading or to what end. Young Vietnamese who worked with the Americans often succumbed to anger or indifference, heightened by a sense of horror at what was happening to the country. Others abandoned themselves to hedonism under the persuasion, easy to come by in South Vietnam, that life was a ghastly joke, and the only way to survive was to drop out.* There was little support for the war, but except for Buddhist youth, little agitation against it. Saigon University, which should have been a seedbed of discontent, was quiet and sleepy, reminiscent of an American university during the Eisenhower years. Vietnamese were not quick to disclose their deepest feelings, but the unmistakable impression was that most young middle-class Vietnamese felt that the war had gone over to the Americans, and they were therefore excused from participation. The Ky government was nowhere popular, except among certain young officers in the army and air force, and among a tough motorcycle-riding cadre of Saigon University students, whose political activities were financed by the prime min-

---

* Marijuana, most of it from Laos, was popular among some elements of the American community and with young Vietnamese who had the money to buy it. Opium was used frequently by the Chinese in Vietnam.

ister's office. They were the committed hell-raising Rockers to the alienated slickly-coiffed Mods. Young educated Vietnamese adopted the stance of despair: there had been so much damage that the country was all but irreparable. The despair reached everywhere, even down to the villages and hamlets, or perhaps particularly to the villages and hamlets. "I am a seller of dreams to people who don't want any," said an American-educated Vietnamese girl.

The intellectuals, and by intellectuals is meant anyone with a decent education who thought seriously about the war, had difficulty being heard. Strict, if sometimes eccentric, censorship of the press prevented a discussion of the issues, and beyond that there were traditional Vietnamese suspicions—of spies, of *agents provocateurs,* of the Americans, the Viet Cong, the French, of the man from the next hamlet, the next village, the next province, of a government waiting to send to the army or to prison any young man who was public in his dissent. Not that dissent, as an American or a European would understand the word, was in the Vietnamese tradition. Vietnamese followed what they called the Mandate of Heaven, which required acceptance of the most harmonious, most "correct," solution. Vietnamese remained uncommitted to the war, because it was not yet decided who was going to win. (Of course, one of the principal reasons it was not "won," at least by the allies, was the refusal of the Vietnamese to commit themselves to it; so it all became a self-fulfilling prophecy of gigantic dimensions.) To commit oneself to the "wrong" side meant to fall from the grace of heaven, to be out of harmony with the universe. Characteristically, many Vietnamese who thought about it tended to blame the Americans—who orchestrated the false note, who caused the disharmony and therefore now bore responsibility for the situation in South Vietnam. A Vietnamese could see it like this:

The Viet Cong had met the Saigon government in a reasonably fair test of arms and ideas and by 1964 by any equable standard had won the war. The Americans arrived in force in 1965 and 1966 and thereby upset all the calculations. Worse, rather than continuing to aid the Saigon government (and thereby continuing, to a degree, the essence of the struggle as one between Vietnamese), the Americans struck out on their own and began to engage the enemy without regard for the regular army of South Vietnam. The North Vietnamese escalated as the Americans escalated and by the end of 1967 there were two basic wars being prosecuted in the country: there were the Americans fighting the main-force North Vietnamese units, and the ARVN fighting the Viet Cong guerrillas. The Vietnamese have a degree of fatalism in their psychology: in a sense, for the Saigon government not to win it on its own (or with aid roughly equal to what Hanoi was supplying the Viet Cong) meant that it would have to lose, *ipso facto.*

The American decision to send combat troops, and all that went with combat troops, was a confusing new element to an uncommitted Vietnamese, who had until then been observing a basically oriental show. At first it could not be believed that the Americans were serious. Vietnamese could not imagine that the United States was prepared to stake its blood, its fortune, and its honor on the outcome of a situation so ambiguous—and one which had been so close to resolution, *i.e.,* the defeat of the Saigon government by the Viet Cong. The equation had to be reworked when the Americans entered the war, and when it was the result looked suspiciously like stalemate, with the Americans not able to lose, but not able to win either. It was not a test of strength or of speed but of endurance, and that seemed true for the population as well as for the combatants.

There were inexplicable lapses in Vietnamese morale, which necessitated patriotic speeches from the leaders of the Saigon government and earnest statements of purpose from the Americans. The Viet Cong, from the available evidence, did not have a serious morale problem. The roots of this are curious, because the logic of the case is that the Americans could not lose the war as a military proposition. Why was it that the population remained indifferent and uncommitted (to put the best face on it) after their government had been joined in battle by the world's most powerful nation? Even after American combat troops arrived in force, Vietnamese were skeptical of the durability of the commitment. All during 1966 and 1967 Vietnamese officials were privately doubting the sincerity of the Johnson Administration—as, in earlier days, they had doubted the Kennedy Administration. "We have to show them that we are in this thing for keeps," Ambassador Lodge said as late as February, 1967. This, with more than 400,000 troops in the country and the American flag nailed squarely to the mast of the Ky government. Or perhaps that was half the trouble. Perhaps the population saw the Americans not as allies in a common enterprise but as a third force not truly, inextricably involved and committed to the country—and therefore, as a practical matter, not decisive in the outcome of the struggle. Too involved in some ways, not involved enough in others, a Vietnamese would say, and shake his head. Morale plunged. (That morale, it will be recalled, was mentioned as an important psychological by-product, and perhaps more than a by-product, of the bombing of North Vietnam. In 1966, it was used as one of the reasons to explain why a bombing pause would be harmful: "What would a pause do to Saigon?" American officials wondered.)

Meanwhile, support for the Viet Cong was . . . problematical. There were rumors of well-dressed teenagers who played tennis in the afternoons and fought in the swamps at night, but these were nowhere substantiated. The Americans assumed that the government, both the civil service and the army, was riddled with spies. To the limited extent that there was any romantic aura about the war, it was the property of the Viet Cong; they were the authentic legatees of the revolutionary tradition. Evidence of the population's admiration for the guerrilla came in odd ways, none odder than the short stories, fiction, which appeared serialized in most of Saigon's twenty or so daily newspapers. Some of the stories were of the *Ladies' Home Journal* variety of domestic tear-jerker, but others were thinly-veiled accounts of the trials and hardships of Viet Cong soldiers. The best known of these was a story entitled "Spring on the Top of a High Mountain," by a popular novelist named Vu Hanh. The story was a sentimental description of four soldiers wandering, and finding love, in the Vietnamese highlands. The soldiers were never identified as Viet Cong, but under the circumstances could hardly have been ARVN. Vu Hanh was arrested on charges of being a Communist (which he almost certainly was not), and arraigned for trial in Saigon. At about the same time as the publication of "Spring on the Top of a High Mountain," the government banned a comic book called *Bich Bop* on the accusation that it, too, was propagandizing for the enemy. But a careful reading and translation of the comic gave another interpretation: the picture-story (badly drawn, with the text laced with obscenities) was straight from *Catch–22*, a world and a war where there were no heroes or villains, only fools. The proper parallel would be the United States in 1944, and it is inconceivable to imagine then popular fiction treating sympathetically the hardships of the Germans or comic books depicting the United States Marines as lazy, stupid and cowardly. But parallels are always dangerous.

Yet young middle-class Vietnamese did not rally to the Viet Cong. It is possible that disgust with the war finally turned into a plague-on-both-your-houses mentality, but it is equally true that the Communist methods were ruthless, their moral code puritanical, their solutions rigidly Marxist, their political objectives laid down in Hanoi; and none of these characteristics were congenial to the easy-going Southerners. Also, the Viet Cong were Communists, and my suspicion is that Communism was as irrelevant to the university students of South Vietnam as it appears to be to students in

America. Thus while being Communist did no particular harm to the cause, it did no particular good either. I cannot produce the captured documents to prove it, but my suspicion is that the Viet Cong, being essentially a peasant movement, was not especially anxious for the support of middle-class students; they were tainted with the manners of the *ancien régime,* as surely as were Catholic Vietnamese. Add to this the snobbish condescension of most urban Vietnamese toward the peasants and it is not difficult to forecast estrangement. Middle-class youth stayed in the universities as long as they could, avoiding military service. Those who had to serve opted for a safe slot in Saigon, a general's aide or an interpreter of English. Of nearly 250 graduates of the military academy at Dalat in 1966, it was said that not more than half a dozen requested a field command; the others all wanted rear echelon posts.

But the appeal of the Viet Cong mystique—the legend of the lone guerrilla in the jungle struggling *for Vietnam*—ought not to be discounted. I once asked a Vietnamese girl from Saigon what kind of man she found most attractive. She replied that her friends like men with good business prospects; or perhaps an educated man, a teacher or writer. We were driving to My Tho, a town about forty miles south of Saigon and were then passing through a village. I pointed out the window of the car and asked her who the girls in the hamlet would find romantic and attractive in South Vietnam. Well, she said with a smile, of course the Viet Cong were very strong around there . . .

THERE were two celebrated confrontations between young Vietnamese intellectuals and high American officials. The first, with Vice President Hubert Humphrey, was described by a participant as very nearly a disaster—owing principally, according to the participant, to Vietnamese distrust of his natural ebullience. The meeting was arranged while Humphrey was in Vietnam following the Honolulu summit conference in early 1966. He stayed two days, visited a pacification project in one of the Saigon slums, and left abruptly. The Vietnamese felt that the vice president did not want to hear complaints. The second meeting, in early 1967 with United Nations Ambassador Arthur Goldberg, was scarcely more successful. The intellectuals (one or two young officials in the Ky government, a teacher, a college professor, several students) argued that the Americans were taking control of the war and therefore of the country, that Vietnamese sovereignty was being subverted, nationalism destroyed, morals ruined. One of the girls repeated a recent incident, in which a GI driving a jeep had crashed into her car. She said that the GI offered no apology, but kept pulling dollar bills out of his pocket and calling her "baby"; she said she did not want money, only an apology. Goldberg replied that these were matters endemic to all wars, and embarked on a rambling anecdote about his personal experiences in North Africa in World War II. For the Vietnamese, it was not a successful answer. In fairness to the ambassador, however, it was often very difficult to talk about the war with young Vietnamese. They tended to view the United States as omnipotent, a rich, wise, powerful father-figure who could be expected to liquidate the war, install a representative civilian government, accomplish the withdrawal of foreign troops, and provide millions, billions if need be, in economic aid—all of it at once, and with no dislocations to South Vietnam. There was no question of gratitude for having saved the nation from Communism.

THERE were young Vietnamese who worked earnestly in the ministries and in the army or for the American civilian organizations whose morale stayed high and whose confidence in victory was unshakable. Some of these sought ways to end the war, or sometimes even to win it, and bring peace to the country. But they were in a minority. Cynicism had become a way of life in Saigon and the large provincial capitals, and the longer the war persisted the more cynical the population became. One of the young Buddhist militants who had taken to the streets under banners calling for an election refused to vote when the government finally agreed to the Buddhist demands, and ordered an election. The election would be rigged, he said; there was no choice to be made between the candidates. Of course the Buddhist had a point (this was the election for a constituent assembly, in September, 1966): while the elections were not "rigged" in a formal sense, it was clear there was very little choice. None of the candidates spoke of the war. The choice in that election was between moderates, between Kennedys and Nixons where the only selection was on the basis of a man's style or his supposed character. In any case, the young Buddhist said, there would be no change in the social or political order as a result of the elections; elections could be held, but nothing would change.

The Vietnamese seemed surprised and puzzled by the inability of the Americans to work their will on the country: surprised, and being Vietnamese, proud in a perverse way. For tiny Vietnam to confound the world's richest, most powerful nation was an event of considerable appeal, especially to a people with a very deep sense of nationalism, if not of nationhood. To appreciate the stalemate was to admire it. And thus, an act of patriotism.

THE MORE the Americans poured into the country, the more the Vietnamese withdrew. The peasants withdrew psychologically, for that was their only means of withdrawal. Others, who had the resources to do so, withdrew in different ways. There was in Saigon a substratum of smart society which tried to live as if there were no war, and which had become, for this and other reasons, more

French than Vietnamese. They spoke French, admired De Gaulle, dressed in the "ye-ye" Paris manner, were bored with Saigon and sick of the struggle. They whiled away noontimes at the *Cercle Sportif* in bright new bikinis bought in the shops on Tu Do Street. They owned bars and pharmacies, or had secured licenses to import goods that Americans wanted. Some were landowners in the Delta or in the provinces north of Saigon where rubber was grown. The farms and plantations were often extensive, and were worked by sharecroppers who were frequently forced to split the yield between the landowner, the Saigon government and the Viet Cong.* The children of rich Vietnamese rode motorcycles or sped around Saigon in two-door Citroëns. If money was offered, draft exemptions could be obtained. As a rule, these Vietnamese stayed away from Americans (except those with whom it was necessary to do business), on the theory that the Americans were at the root of the trouble — "the trouble," in this case, being "the situation in Vietnam," the cause of their own estrangement. Occasionally some of the girls, who traveled in groups, would appear at an American cocktail party, but not often. You would see them at the *Arc En Ciel*, the Chinese restaurant in Cholon, and sometimes at the Phu Tho race track. The members of the Vietnamese smart set were far from tragic figures, but they were among the displaced in the country. There were many displaced and these were perhaps the least deserving of sympathy or understanding, but they were a part of what

---

* The land problem was a cruel one for the peasant. Viet Cong taxes were higher than government taxes, but in Viet Cong territory the peasant was formally given title to the land. Under the Saigon government, taxes were lower but the landlords returned to assert their titles and demand rent. It was said that if the peasant had a choice between owning his own land and paying high taxes on it or not owning his land and paying low taxes (but high rent), he would of course opt for the former. No mystery there, or in the reluctance of the peasant to embrace the Saigon government. The Saigon government meant landlords, and the Sheriff of Nottingham.

Saigon had become. After the Americans had left and the war ended, they would remain.

This is really a story about Aimée, who had come to Saigon from Paris via Teheran. She had stopped in Teheran to see Isfahan and Darius's Palace at Persepolis, and intended to stay in Vietnam just long enough to conduct personal business. Her visa was valid for four weeks, her business would take her three, and when it was done she planned to return to her flat in Paris. In the meantime she would look around and see old friends. Aimée became a part of the *Cercle Sportif* scene for a few weeks in the fall of 1966.

She was what the Saigon smart set called a *coloniste,* one of the 30,000 Vietnamese living in Paris. She was twenty-two, lovely and shy and quiet, with dark hair cut very short, European-style. She traveled on a French passport, skied in the Austrian Alps in the winter, and spent part of the summer at Cannes. She lived in Paris and modeled for a living. Her English was excellent, spoken softly with a trace of a British accent that set her apart in Saigon. Aimée said her principal interest in life was art, thus the stops at Isfahan and Persepolis; but now she was a Vietnamese in Saigon, returned to her country for the first time in six years.

No, she did not follow the war closely in Paris, although many of the other Vietnamese there did. There were political parties and Vietnamese cafés, and intellectuals to comment on what was happening. One of the most prominent of these lived in Geneva, but sometimes visited Paris. Articles and books were written and television was full of the travail of Vietnam. Aimée read *Le Monde* and *Figaro,* but mostly for the art and cinema reviews. She was not involved in Saigon. It was very far away from Europe. While there was a great deal of talking about the war, very few Paris Vietnamese, including some of the most talented of the society, wanted to come back. Paris was not always congenial, but the war was worse.

Aimée spent most of her days at the *Cercle Sportif,* with its shade trees, swimming pool and tennis courts. In the evenings after a game of tennis it was pleasant to sit on the veranda sipping a drink, and comment on the form of the players. The club was the retreat of the French during colonial days, but now the membership was more representative. The French did not have to hear the sound of tumbrels in Tu Do Street to know that club policies would have to be liberalized, so not long ago the doors eased open. Membership was now said to be about one-third French, one-third Vietnamese or Chinese, and one-third American. The Americans seemed to predominate.

The French appeared on the weekends, in from their rubber plantations in Tay Ninh and Long Khanh. The plantations were working, but not well; taxes had to be paid all around, and labor was difficult to find. It was not unusual for half the work force to disappear, then return at a later date, with no explanation. But the French managed to survive. They were the Swiss of Vietnam, and some said more than Swiss. They kept to themselves as a hedge against involvement, for they were under attack both from the Ky government and the Americans. I think the Americans in South Vietnam disliked the French even more than they disliked the Vietnamese. In conversations with Americans the French were always polite, and noncommittal; they never mentioned the progress of the war. But they always seemed to be smiling.

Each day sometime between noon and two o'clock (the times shifted to confuse potential assassins) Henry Cabot Lodge of Massachusetts, accompanied by a bodyguard, would come to sun himself, eat a light lunch, and chug a slow crawl from one end of the pool to the other, deep to shallow. He was watched with great interest by the Vietnamese girls at poolside. Lodge was one of two authentic Saigon celebrities. The other was General Westmoreland.

The Vietnamese at the *Cercle Sportif* gossiped in French and drank *citron pressé* soda in the heat of the afternoon before returning to their businesses. They led a schizophrenic life, but managed to endure. Money made it possible. Inflation was growing at the rate of 50 percent a year, so the money had continually to be reinvested; much of it went for the construction of apartment houses. But there were large sums which went to bank accounts abroad and all rich Vietnamese considered quitting the country. Those who left with their new clothes and $5,000 passport and fistful of dollars went to Paris. But in Saigon or in Paris they were refugees, neither wholly Vietnamese nor wholly European. The country was still there, and still at war; men were still dying. And no Vietnamese was happy in exile. A Vietnamese, whether Catholic or Buddhist, Hoa Hao, Cao Dai, Confucian or whatever, believed that Vietnam was paradise, although naturally the war deferred everything. They were not in any case comfortable in the company of other Vietnamese who had chosen to place themselves in the center of the struggle. And those Vietnamese who did, particularly the young, had very little use for those who did not, particularly the exiles.

AT DINNER parties in Saigon attempts were made to lead conversations away from the war. There was some talk of books, children, food, sex, life on the outside, events in America, Europe, China, anywhere; but it was rarely successful. No one could forget what it was that had brought them to Vietnam in the first place. Its only reason for existence was the war. The war closed in and if you lived in Saigon you were drawn into its vortex. Someone would mention the state of the pacification program in Binh Dinh or the kidnapping of the village chief of Loc Tien, or the death of a friend near Danang, and attention was turned back to Vietnam. It always happened. Certain women, both Vietnamese and American, learned to live with it, as one learns to live with a disability. Others thrived on it, as an escape from personal matters. But most did not, and their attention wandered and their eyes glazed as the conversation moved inexorably from vacations in Bali to the casualties at An Khe.

Aimeé, the girl from Paris, listened quietly one night at dinner and cautiously answered questions about the Vietnamese in Paris. She became interested briefly when someone said there were no heroes in South Vietnam. There were no war heroes or peace heroes or culture heroes; only, to those so inclined, Ho Chi Minh. There was not even a Vietnamese Jean-Paul Belmondo. Or Albert Camus. It was an army of Schweiks and Yossarians, cowards and fools, mostly fools. Could a country exist without heroes? Aimée, the exile, said it could not. She lit a cigarette then, took two hesitant puffs, and put it out. She did not smoke again, having remembered that a proper Vietnamese girl did not smoke cigarettes. The other girls at the table did not.

Two of these were from Hanoi, and had come with their Catholic families south to Saigon in the late nineteen-forties. The talk at the table had turned from heroes to the persistence of the war and the endurance of the people. The girl who was giving the dinner party had put a recording of Amalia Rodrigues, the Portuguese fado singer, on the record player. The wine went around the table again, and the girls told what it was like in Hanoi at the beginning of the struggle.

Though their families were educated and rich, they lived in caves outside the city during the worst of it, when there were shellings and mortar attacks. Ho Chi Minh's people eventually killed half a million Vietnamese in the process of consolidating the revolution. But the early deaths were the responsibility of the French, whose twilight struggle in the cause of colonialism went on for eight years. The girls' fathers were non-Communist Viet Minh and dedicated to the expulsion of the French from Vietnam. It was very bad in North Vietnam in the late nineteen-forties. "Every night we went to the top of the hill and looked toward the lights of Hanoi, because that's where our hearts were," one of the girls said.

Now the Vietnamese existed day to day as in a cave, she went on. Some retired altogether, although the country was at war. Most Vietnamese refused to risk anything because so much had been risked already and nothing had been gained. The war endured along with the people. The French had left and now the Americans had come, one colonial regime for another, and still the war went on. There were many dead, and no change or improvement to show for the dead. Vietnam was dead, and there was nothing that would bring it back. So a man tended his flower garden and wandered about his house absorbed in books recounting early Vietnamese history, the glorious part. The man once had been a judge, but he no longer read law books.

All of this was said in the low quiet singsong of polite conversation. The girl had been to the United States and had received a college education. She could have remained, with her perfect English and French and quick intelligence. She chose to return to Vietnam to work first for the government, and finally for the Americans. The decision had been an act of will. She had come to dinner from work, which was with the refugees outside Saigon, and was dressed in what she called her schoolteacher's uniform: a plain white *ao dai*, frayed at the edges, with her hair done in a bun on the back of her head.

The Vietnamese girl from Paris had said nothing, and when someone asked her how things had changed in Vietnam in six years she replied shyly that she wasn't sure. There was less war then, and fewer Americans, and not so many dead, and perhaps more cheer than now. Diem was president, and Diem's brother Nhu was running the secret police. But it was six years ago. She was being very careful, because the other girls were watching her with hawks' eyes and hard expressions. Saigon was so crowded now. Have you ever seen such traffic jams? And she was told that rice prices were up, which made it difficult for the peasants and the poor people in the cities . . . But she had been a schoolgirl the last time, absorbed in books and anxious to make an impression on her classmates at Marie Curie lycée. So few of her family were left in Vietnam; she had gone with her mother and father, and there was now only a grandmother, who lived in the village where she was born. She said she did not know much of Vietnam now. She lived in France.

THE VIETNAMESE atmosphere, both of the people and of the land, varied from province to province and region to region. What held true in one part of the country was irrelevant in another. So it was with Saigon and Hue, which was the capital of Central Vietnam, the seat of the Vietnamese emperors of the past two thousand years. One of the grander schemes of the late President Ngo Dinh Diem was to transform Hue into a tourist center, with expensive hotels and boat rides up the Perfumed River. He never succeeded, for there were intervening events and more urgent business, but the idea was sound. Some millennia hence, when the archaeologists are searching for fragments of the Vietnamese civilization, one hopes they dig at Hue. It is virtually the only large Vietnamese city untouched, by the war or the Americans.

Hue was and is the hub of political and cultural Vietnam, as contrasted with Saigon, the center of commercial and bureaucratic Vietnam. There were no real politics in Saigon, just ministries and disenfranchised political leaders who talked long in cafés. In Hue there were political organizations like the Dai Viet (Greater Vietnam Party) and the V.N.Q.D.D. (Vietnam Quoc Dan Dang, or Vietnamese kuo-mintang, modeled on the Sun Yat-sen organization) and followers as well as leaders. The most potent force was Buddhism, and the most potent leader—political, religious, and cultural—was the ascetic monk, Thich Tri Quang. In Vietnam a political activist might belong to a half-dozen political tendencies (as the word was translated from Vietnamese to French to English), making coherent political analysis very difficult. Central Vietnam was the home of the heavyweight politicians: Ngo Dinh Diem grew up in Hue, Ho Chi Minh in a village near Quang Ngai.

During the Buddhist rebellion in 1966, Hue scarcely seemed a part of South Vietnam at all. In the evenings you bicycled past seditious banners calling for the overthrow of the government and expulsion of the foreigners, past the sound of martial music and shouted slogans, to the north side of the slowly-flowing Perfumed River. The sampans were moored there, up-river beyond the town center. For two hundred piasters ($1.50), you rented a sampan to sleep in. You brought your own wine and were provided with pillows and blankets. If you were unlucky, the people in the sampan next door had a transistor radio, which would be tuned to the fluty shriek of oriental music. You were paddled to the middle of the river, listening to the chatter of the people in the other sampans; an anchor was dropped and the family decorously retired to the rear. You fell asleep in the middle of the river, the night silence disturbed only briefly by artillery fire from the United States Marine base at Phu Bai, eight miles south of town.

There were only a few cars in town, apart from the military jeeps, which made it a quiet city compared to Saigon. Late at night in a bicycle-rickshaw all you could hear was the swish-swish of the rubber tires on the pavement as the bike glided along the streets, lit only by little puddles of light from electric lamps. It was a place to sit out-of-doors with a glass of cold beer and look at the river and smoke a cigarette, watching the smoke rise in a straight line in the light heat of nighttime. It was then that you could have a soft and slow-moving discussion about things of no importance. There was very little night life and the war seemed far away.

The town was eventually declared off-limits to American troops, except the officers and men of the small MACV advisory team assigned to the 1st ARVN Division, which was billeted outside of town. Even when it was on-limits, leave was restricted to one hundred GI's (in this case, Marines) a day, who were requested to be back at their base by five P.M. There were thirty-three bars, most of them kept out of sight, when the town was on-limits and open to soldiers. After certain incidents, many of them sexual, between the bar girls and the GI's, the town was closed. The MACV compound on the Phu Bai road leading into the center of town was surrounded by barbed wire and lit by floodlights at night. The compound seemed offensive and out of place in Hue, an obscene reminder of American nervousness and vulnerability. But by early 1967 Viet Cong guerrillas would enter the city by night, and the Americans figured they needed all the protection they could get. There were a number of assassinations that year, and security in Hue plunged. The population was not especially friendly to begin with and became openly hostile after the Buddhist upheaval. For a time, American officers were not sure of the loyalties of the 1st ARVN Division. The Division without doubt opposed the Saigon government, as it proved by a near-mutiny in mid-spring, 1966.* What worried the Americans, though, was whether or not it was anti-South; that is, not to put too fine a point on it, pro-North.

It was possible in Hue to see the grace and quality of Vietnamese life (for those who could afford it) unencumbered by the war or the influx of Americans. There were low hills, the river, and a pastel sky, meandering streets and silence. The province chief lived not in a barbed-wire compound but in a stone mansion by the river, a large

---

* The incident resulted in long-lasting bitterness between the Marines and the Vietnamese in I Corps. A one point in the rebellion the ARVN abandoned its garrison, leaving it open to plunder by the Viet Cong. The Communists attacked (or simply walked in) and carried off substantial quantities of supplies, including artillery shells, grenades and dynamite. Later, as Marine casualties from mines and booby traps grew, one colonel remarked angrily that, "we're getting all that ARVN stuff back now, one by one."

villa with a circular driveway and a collection of paintings and sculpture inside. Directly opposite the province chief's house, across the river, was the Citadel, the palace copied from the Imperial Palace at Peking by the French puppet emperor Bao Dai (who is still alive, living with some fanfare on the French Riviera). Marine civil affairs officers used to take the troops to the Citadel to give them an idea of Vietnamese culture, an instructive lesson for infantrymen just back from the Demilitarized Zone or the dangerous hamlets near Route One, Bernard Fall's Street Without Joy, fifteen miles north. They looked like tourists, walking slowly and awkwardly over the grounds, being lectured by a tough major reading from a USAID handbook. On the grounds of the Citadel one found exquisite lily ponds and a throne room, and gardens that seemed ordered up for the pages of *National Geographic* magazine. Just beyond the walls, and the moat surrounding the walls, stands a fine museum built of teak and containing gongs. The atmosphere is ordered, the air scented.

A quarter of a mile from the palace, down a rutted dirt road that runs along the river, Sister Isabella and Sister Florence ran the Kim Long Orphanage and Insane Asylum. It is a small and neat collection of buildings beside a well-kept church which dominates a grove of trees. The orphanage and the madhouse are well away from the town center, and enclosed by a fence. The inmates are mostly Catholic refugees from North Vietnam, but a few were badly maimed victims of the war. Prime Minister Ky and his wife once made an inspection tour of Kim Long, where the orphans weave baskets to sell in the market and blankets for the insane to lie on. They were accompanied by the mayor of Hue and the corps commander and a score of lesser officials, all with their wives. Kim Long was not on the normal VIP route in Hue; the impression was that Sister Isabella and Sister Florence were not used to guests. The mayor and the corps commander were not frequent visitors.

The procession commenced at the church and moved through the buildings until it came to the playroom of the orphanage. It was an evil-smelling, ill-lit playroom without toys, except for an old metal jungle gym in one corner and a few broken dolls which littered the floor. The madhouse was in the building adjoining it, and from it came the shrieks and yells of the insane. Ky and his wife went straight in and stooped down to pat the children, many of whom were covered with raw sores. The prime minister was relaxed and talked with Sister Isabella as the children scrambled around his legs. He seemed not to mind, and frequently smiled at the children. The other men, the mayor and the corps commander and the others, stayed outside the room, smoking and talking among themselves. Ky's wife was in the middle of the room watching the children. The other ladies hung back, their faces blank and unforgiving, holding the delicate skirts of the *ao dai* above their ankles. When two little children broke from the jungle gym and headed toward them, they moved farther back, out of the doorway. An idiot child scuttled across the floor like a crab and stretched out an arm to touch a silk-stockinged leg, and the leg pulled back slowly as you would pull a bone out of a dog's reach.

Sister Isabella and Sister Florence had very little money and were plagued, as was all Vietnam, by a shortage of doctors. There were three hundred inmates of all categories in Kim Long. The sick and the mad did not get the attention they needed. At the end of the tour both nuns were given thick envelopes filled with money by Ky and his wife. The two nuns bowed low in thanks.

ACROSS Le Loi Street from the Hue Hotel, and just down from Dong Khanh girls' school, stood the *Cercle Sportif* of Hue, a large, rambling stone building with tennis courts and a swimming pool and a river in back. Small sailing craft were tethered to the dock.

The black leather chairs inside were mostly empty in the spring of 1966, owing to the political crisis. It was not considered politic to go skylarking around the *Cercle Sportif* as the government in Saigon shuddered. The list of members on the bulletin board in the foyer contained French as well as Vietnamese names. There were one or two American names.

The aged Vietnamese patron explained one day that the club was the center of activity in town, with a lively ambiance and sports and games. It was something of an intellectual center as well, and catered to students and faculty of Hue University. The reading room, with subscriptions to all the French and Vietnamese newspapers, had backgammon boards and playing cards and was always full. "But now, you see, the only people who come here are the foreign journalists and others . . ." The patron paused from embarrassment—not that he wished to offend the foreign journalists, you understand. It is just that things were not now as they had been.

The University of Hue was the best in Vietnam, with a better faculty than Saigon or Can Tho or the military academy at Dalat. It is difficult to say whether it is, or was, better than the University of Hanoi, but the presumption is that it was. Life in Hue was more serious. The university was a group of low-slung buildings built in the colonial manner, with porches and wide windows to let in the breeze. The aspect was antiseptic, like a hospital complex, probably because there were no students about and the only sound was a desultory typewriter clacking away in the administration building. The students were all downtown at Buddhist headquarters, or home for the holiday. Bui Tuong Hoan, the rector of the university, talked that day about the future of Vietnam. Hoan was a thin, restless, precise man in his mid-thirties, somewhat haughty in manner and indignant over the government's actions against Hue and against the university. The rector in that spring of 1966 saw a twenty-year war, but one which would never be one until the people became engaged. In that academic atmosphere it was possible to talk in theories rather than facts, to forget for a moment the body counts and weapons counts and concentrate instead on the tone of the struggle.

Hoan said that the people would not become engaged until they saw the war as their war. Now they saw it as an American war in which the Vietnamese people were the pawns. It was a war between the Americans and the Chinese being fought in Vietnam; the Vietnamese had no real part to play except to offer the stage. The Saigon government was an American surrogate, set up to cover the prosecution of an American war which had as its aim the containment of China. In the process the Vietnamese were offered up in sacrifice. Foreign influence and foreign domination disturbed Hoan more than Ho Chi Minh's battalions, and he came very close to saying that in a choice between subjugation by other Vietnamese or subjugation by the Americans, he would choose the other Vietnamese whatever their political coloration. Abruptly then he turned to the question of American policy, and demanded: What do you Americans want?* Do you want negotiations? A fight to the finish? Why do you support a puppet government? Ky and Thieu have no authority here. Why are they supported?

Conservative circles in Saigon would call Hoan a crypto-Communist, and those circles may have been right. But it seemed more likely to me that he was an old-fashioned leftist nationalist xenophobe, in despair over the course of the war. Not, given the vehemence of Hoan's views, that it made very much difference. In any case, as the interview ended he said that the war was Saigon's affair.

Hoan recommended long chats with Buddhist student leaders, particularly Buu Ton, the law student who was running the struggle

---

* This was a favorite ploy of exasperated Vietnamese. I once heard an equally exasperated American diplomat give the perfect answer: "Win the goddamned war."

in Hue. Buddhist headquarters, in the center of Hue, had all the trappings of a Latin American or Middle Eastern revolutionary headquarters: martial music and hot-tempered speeches, young men with weapons, and the infectious excitement of a movement. There were long delays until an interview could be arranged. Vietnam, Buu Ton said in hesitant English, had become the American Spain, with nothing in it for the Vietnamese except to fight and die. For themselves, they opted out—or "struggled." Ton and the other student leaders were being careful about anti-American statements, but the implications were obvious. They were equally vehement about denying any connections with the Viet Cong. But when the movement collapsed many of the young student leaders disappeared and were presumed to have joined the Communists. They wanted the war ended, and they wanted the Saigon government out. They could not recommend a suitable successor, but stressed that whoever he was he must have the "confidence of the people."

There was at this time a good deal of guessing over what percentage of university students in Hue were engaged in the rebellion. A satisfactory figure for either the students or the population at large was never reached, but it seemed clear to me that Ton and the others had struck a very deep chord in the Vietnamese, particularly Vietnamese youth who did not feel a part of what the war was supposed to be about, nor especially anxious to die for what they regarded as American foreign policy objectives.

Later, listening to the click of billiard balls on smooth felt tables under slowly turning fans at the sporting club, one worried the problem with a young Saigonese, a medical student at the university, and his wife. They had just come in from a sail on the river and were sitting, shoes off and relaxed, drinking Coca-Cola. The medical student's attitudes were rather more detached than those of the Buddhists at Struggle Committee headquarters and of the university rector. No one knew what the Buddhist leaders wanted, the student said. The whole business was fouled up and no one could tell what would happen until Tri Quang came to power, which he surely would. The Buddhists were experts at causing trouble, and their discontent was perennial. It did not, in that sense, matter whether the grievances were real or imagined. True or false, they were serious. But the situation was not. It was just politics, and in any case no more than a quarter of the student body was really interested. The student from Saigon said that everyone wanted the war to end.

The student was asked where he intended to practice when he finished medical school. He looked around the *Cercle Sportif du Hue* and smiled and said he planned to go to America, where he understood there was a need for physicians.

5

RUFF-PUFFS, AIR AND ARTY, AND OTHER EXOTICS

THE COUNTRY was overrun with armed men, both ours and theirs. Everybody had a weapon in Vietnam, and Lodge used to say that the greatest problem after the war was ended and the Communists defeated would be to disarm the population. He half suspected that the Communists were bandits first and Marxists second, and there was some evidence to support that view. The country was treated, in any case, like an armed camp. Part of the problem stemmed from the regular reorganizations of the Vietnamese armed forces. It became inevitable that the Vietnamese military establishment would become not unlike the American. But what could be tolerated in an immensely rich and generally pacific nation of 200 million people created serious internal tensions in a poor, generally warlike collection of provinces of about 15 million people.

The Vietnamese believed in diversity. There was, first of all, the regular ARVN—buffered, as it were, by elite units of Marines, Rangers and paratroopers. These were under different commanders, who responded sometimes well, sometimes badly, sometimes not at all, to orders from above. Below the regular battalions were the Regional Forces, which technically were under the control of the province chief, and the Popular Forces, which were under the control of the district chief. They were security forces, local militiamen meant to defend and keep the peace. The bureaucratic, and therefore not very useful, parallel with the United States would be the state police and the county sheriff's office, laced with the National Guard. Below the RF's and the PF's (collectively known as Ruff-Puffs) were regular national police, white-suited, pistol-carrying cops known as White Mice, under the direction of Brigadier General Loan, and something called the Police Field Force. The function of the PFF was never clear to me, nor I think to most Americans in Vietnam; it was simply another irregular group, like the Armed Combat Youth, whose responsibilities were likewise a mystery. But they all were armed, and more or less dangerous. Off to the right—if this were an organization chart—were the cadre, the 59-man teams which were thrust into the hamlets to act as social workers and civil defense forces, to build roads and erect defenses and teach the population to defend themselves and give their loyalty to the Saigon government. Off the chart completely were the Provincial Reconnaissance Units, elsewhere called counterterror teams, which "brought the war to the Cong's backyard," as one colonel put it. The PRU's were run by the CIA, and had a remarkable record (particularly in the Delta) of successful terrorism. One problem was their delight in decapitation, and then displaying the results before American television cameras. One such display almost ended their activities in the province of Long An. But they were kept on after the PRU leader explained that his men were about the only troops in Long An who apparently enjoyed fighting the enemy. That was the highest recommendation you could give in Vietnam, and so the PRU's were told to stay away from Americans with cameras.

It is almost impossible, and anyway not very useful, to give a description of the various strategies employed by these forces. They varied from province to province, depending on the capacities of the commander and his unit. Certain Ranger commands in the vicinity of Saigon were there to guard against *coups d'état,* and never moved against the Viet Cong. The Vietnamese paratroopers enjoyed staging elaborate jumps in the Delta. An American major once told me that the paras were the best troops in Vietnam, but never got any publicity; he said that if the war were left to the paras, there would be no Viet Cong. I never heard any comment, this way or that, about the Marines. One Ranger unit stationed near An Khe had as its principal function supplying the men of the American 1st Cavalry Division with prostitutes, beer and ice.

THE MOST appealing troops in Vietnam were the Ruff-Puffs—the Regional and Popular Forces. Dressed in a grab-bag collection of uniforms, they ranged in age from sixteen to sixty-five. Recruitment procedures were bizarre and amenities unknown. They had no help: indifferent leadership, ancient weapons, inadequate pay, dreadful housing, and absolutely no motivation to do what they were doing, which was risking their lives fighting an enemy superior in every respect. The only advantage to membership in these forces was that if you were in the Popular Force you could live at home and if you were in the Regional Force you could have your family with you. The PF's guarded the villages and hamlets, and the RF's were assigned to the districts (although they frequently moved throughout the province). It was an army of family men, reflected in the pay scales: about 2,000 piasters a month ($18) plus 700 piasters each for wife and children. The wonder was that no matter how abominably these men were treated they always remained cheerful. Their objective was to walk as slowly as possible and try not to damage anything, to stay away from the Viet Cong and steal a chicken or two if it was possible. Some regular battalions of the ARVN went through villages and hamlets like Attila the Hun; but not the Ruff-Puffs. It was not much of an outfit with which to be identified because no one took it seriously. In villages the women and children laughed at them, and in Saigon they were ignored. They were really terrible troops.

It was infrequent that the Ruff-Puffs ever left their forts. They were not assigned to "search and destroy," in the portentous phrase of the American military, but to protect. The trouble was that in the Delta, for example, practically everything was vulnerable, and as often as not the Viet Cong would assault the forts and drive the defenders out, usually inflicting heavy casualties. As a rule the Ruff-Puffs were badly disciplined, although no one doubted their fighting qualities as men. What they lacked was any plausible reason for doing what they were doing. More often than not the local leaders negotiated what became known as an accommodation. This took the form of a nonaggression pact with the Viet Cong. On the other side of My Tho, the pretty little market town about forty miles south of Saigon, there was physical evidence of the agreement: a well-traveled path not fifty yards from the fort, which the guerrillas used as a highway to move men and supplies.

The forts which the Ruff-Puffs were meant to defend were relics of the French occupation. They were mostly built of mud and concrete that looked like mud. The families were housed in the rear, and at all times of day and night rice was cooking in scarred black pots. Children ran loose and the defenders lounged against the guard posts and dozed. When siesta time came, they slept. They hoped the enemy would stay away. If by chance there was an attack, the defenders could expect no help, even though there might be an ARVN battalion nearby. There had been too many occasions when a relief column was ambushed, as it sped up the road to reinforce a beleaguered squad of Ruff-Puffs; so ARVN officers barred night activity, which in a war is a little like a morning newspaper refusing to print afternoon news. The Ruff-Puffs sat in their forts terrified, with reason, and took heavy losses when attacked. Life in the forts tended to be nasty, brutish and short. Because there were so many casualties, the Vietnamese officers and their American advisers were uneasy whenever the Ruff-Puffs were on patrol, and in a position of engagement with the enemy. The Ruff-Puffs were always under-strength, with some "companies" barely reaching fifty men. For the Regional and Popular Forces, the problem was survival.

But they went about it with a certain *élan,* and among some units military maneuvers became a game. One of the best afternoons I ever had in Vietnam was in the company of a band of Ruff-Puffs commanded by a veteran fighter named Tran Huyen Hiep, a second lieutenant in the RF who sported a goatee, a black beret, a rakish bamboo swagger stick, and an immense .38 caliber revolver. He was standing in the middle of a rice paddy smoking a Lark and yawning. His French-made sunglasses, black-rimmed with yellow lenses, glinted in the sun. Tran Huyen Hiep was trying to figure out how to proceed, in the face of what he considered to be an overwhelming force of Communist terrorists. I had watched the preliminaries:

From the forward bunker of the gray mud fort, through the slit hole and the barbed wire beyond, the American colonel had peered intently at the motionless horizon. His Vietnamese counterpart, a trim, reedy man in knife-creased fatigues, spoke carefully over a field telephone. The colonel could not understand what was being said. Two miles beyond the fort, a company of Regional Forces, re-inforced by a twenty-man platoon of Popular Forces, had reported contact with the enemy. The troops were out of sight, beyond three tree lines and the muddy paddies that made up the battleground in the Delta. A rain had passed that morning, leaving the ricefields spongy. The sun baked the mud and the heat rose in fetid waves.

The company of RF and the platoon of PF had begun a conventional sweep that morning, working out from the elaborate American radar installation on the outskirts of My Tho, retracing ground covered the day before by a battalion of ARVN. Now these particular Ruff-Puffs were bogged down in a stand of trees two miles south of the fort. The American colonel and the Vietnamese major were tense and on edge, as they took turns on the field telephone. The colonel would speak, then stride nervously up and down the trench, looking anxiously south. They were both trying to figure out what was happening. There was no gunfire, so it was probable that the force had run into a single sniper. But no one knew. "There could be as many as two hundred VC out there," the colonel said. Tension inside the fort was running high.

The telephone communications with the Ruff-Puffs, and with Hiep, were unsatisfactory. A young American captain and two sergeants offered to leave the fort and join the company, ostensibly to find out what was going on, but also to lend a hand in case there was a fight. The colonel and the major agreed that it might be a good idea, and the three soldiers and I set off. After thirty minutes of traversing ricefields we came upon the force, sprawled under palm trees eating lunch. And Hiep commanding the rice paddy, worrying.

The officers and men had liberated half a dozen chickens, boiled them in a large black pot, and were ladling out soup over rice. They instantly offered—or insisted—that we share the lunch. There was a good deal of laughter when one of the Americans was served a webbed foot. In fact, there was a good deal of laughter period. In the distance, artillery was firing and as the guns boomed the men sat back and ate the chicken and giggled. It was all but consumed when from the left flank came a roar of gunfire. Hiep, swagger stick aloft, bawled for the mortar and began shouting into the field telephone. But he had mistaken the swagger stick for the telephone and it was a minute before the two instruments became disentangled.

Then from a jacket pocket he extracted a map of the My Tho quadrant (in English and Vietnamese) and a sheaf of documents, presumably codes. He was manhandling the phone between his shoulder and cheekbone with one hand and sorting out the maps and documents with the other.

The troops, rushing forward in a long, laughing, uneven line struck out for a dike fifty yards distant. Hiep hung back, gleefully bellowing into the telephone for artillery support. Artillery fire was the first rung on the ladder of escalation in South Vietnam (or, if you prefer, the initial tumbling domino). The second rung was a fighter-bomber air strike. The third was a pounding from giant eight-engined Guam-based B–52 bombers, as they were called by correspondents in Saigon. There was no chance for a B–52 strike; none at all. But if it was possible to call in the artillery from My Tho, by convincing superior officers that large numbers of the aggressor enemy were entrenched in the tree line, then it was equally possible to engage the interest of the authorities at Can Tho. Can Tho was the air base farther south. It was possible, if the hand was played well and boldly, that he, Tran Huyen Hiep, could negotiate an air strike.

It could be a delicious moment. Intelligence had long suspected a main-force Viet Cong unit of operating in that very rice paddy. Hiep's forward sentinels had excitedly reported firing from the tree line. Ten shots had been exchanged (no dead, no wounded, no missing) and when I jokingly suggested that if you squared ten you got one hundred, there was nodding assent. One of the Vietnamese giggled and translated for Hiep. From then on it seemed to become an established fact. "There are one hundred VC in the tree line," Hiep repeated over the field telephone.

The American advisers were solemn, gravely considering the possibilities. The battlefield was now silent, but that was no guarantee for the future, where the hated Cong were everywhere and anxious to pounce. "Charlie hit them once and moved off into the tree line," said the American captain. "Charlie has got maybe one hundred guys and we have got one hundred and ten, and you don't assault a dug-in position. Savvy?"

It seemed plausible enough, and Hiep was in enthusiastic agreement. The tempo of the battle had slowed and the men had laid down their arms and were napping under the shade trees of the little grove we called the Command Post. It was siesta hour (or, as it turned out, two hours). There was no firing anywhere now, but as if by telepathy the first few peasants were beginning to emerge from the far ricefield. They were walking slowly toward the grove where we sat, many of them carrying heavy loads on their backs. As they passed and moved on they smiled politely and made small gestures of welcome. One old man with a long wispy beard and sunken cheeks looked exactly like Ho Chi Minh. The peasants were clearing out their homes which, as it happened, lay just beyond the tree line. Apparently they knew what was coming.

Three kilometers away there sat a full battalion of ARVN infantry, combat-ready. It was not clear then and is not clear now why that battalion was not summoned and flung into the battle. But it was not. There were no explanations why. Hiep was on the phone again, pleading for an air strike. The artillery had not responded. Now he was in a ricefield with 110 men facing a tree line bristling with the aggressor enemy. In the heat of midday, the chicken gone, his infantry taking a siesta, Hiep ambled about the paddy brandishing his swagger stick, talking into the telephone, consulting his maps and documents, and gesturing menacingly at the tree line.

Can Tho capitulated. There was a surge of enthusiasm when the first American aircraft appeared. They were 1,800-mile-an-hour Phantom F–4C's, the pride of the American Air Force. They are beautiful lethal machines idling slowly, orbiting at 2,000 feet, the engines of one million pounds' thrust roaring in the distance, circling the targets. The engines make a brutal sound, more blast than roar; angrier and nastier than one million bees.

The Phantoms cost $2 million each, and are celebrated for their work over North Vietnam. Droop-nosed, two torpedo-shaped jet engines melded into the fuselage, they carry cannon and bombs, napalm and white phosphorus. They circled majestically three times before they went in for the first of dozens of passes. Hiep and his band cheered as the first load of bombs went crashing into the huts just beyond the tree line, five hundred yards away. Hiep was transported, flailing the swagger stick to the rhythm of the jets diving, climbing, leveling, and diving again as the explosions reached a crescendo. The five-hundred-pound bombs blasted deep holes in the forest. Chunks of earth and houses were blown into the air three hundred feet, then twirled down, disintegrating into small bits as they fell. There was no answering ground fire. There was no indication that any Viet Cong were hiding in the tree line, or beyond it.

The strike had taken more than an hour to arrange and during this time farm families had come in little groups of two and three out of the tree line. The children came to the grove of palm trees to watch the air strike, turning their heads like spectators at a tennis match as the jets idled slowly, heeled over beautifully as gulls seen from the deck of a ship, and dived and destroyed their homes. As the Phantoms pressed the attack, the children began to lose interest; they asked the Americans for chewing gum and cigarettes—"chugum" and "sahlem," meaning Salems, the menthol cigarette coveted by the Vietnamese. Hiep stood commandingly on a little knoll, watching the progress of his air strike, and talking confidentially into the telephone. He might have been a stockbroker speaking to a client as he watched the numbers on the ticker tape: one explosion was on target, another a little off, a third half a ricefield away, and Hiep, nodding and smiling, would comment on each one. With each explosion, there was a ripple of excitement. But the children were not overwhelmed. They saw air strikes with approximately the same frequency as an American child sees parades, if the American child lives on a parade route. These children lived in what is called a free strike zone, a zone which may be freely struck with bombs.

There were three flights of three planes each. They were followed by armed helicopters, which chewed up the jungle with machine guns. Many of the soldiers continued to slumber, occasionally raising themselves on one elbow to watch the bombs fall. There was no answering fire from the tree line and now Hiep was commencing to send out a patrol to learn what, if anything, had happened to the Cong.

It was a moment of great drama and great style. Were the Communists concealed in ambush behind trees? Had the bombs done their work? Was it a *trap?* Hiep stood in the middle of the paddy smoking the Lark and pointing with the swagger stick, consulting the maps and papers, and shouting into the telephone. At a verbose command his men, smiling and jostling one another, struggled to their feet. Then, Hiep in the lead, they ambled across the field to the tree line. After he had gone about a dozen yards, the commander turned again to face the Americans. *"Au revoir,"* he cried, and resumed the march into an empty ricefield.

IT WAS somehow more serious with the Americans, and the judgments tended to be harder. Most of the Americans worked and lived in a world quite apart from the Vietnamese. The antic aspects of life with the Ruff-Puffs or with the PRU's did not work when applied to the Americans. It came out high tragedy and sometimes farce, rarely high comedy. Sometimes all an observer could do was lay out the available facts, repeat that they were probably incomplete, and say: look, this is what sometimes happens. Draw me a moral. Tell me about armed men, artillery and air strikes.

In May of 1966 battalions of the 1st Infantry Division were operating on the fringes of the sprawling Michelin rubber plantations,
about fifty miles northwest of Saigon. It was in Binh Duong
province. This was before the huge multi-division operations were
assembled in War Zone C and the area called the Iron Triangle.
These first operations were probes around the edges, to test enemy
strength and to get a feel for the terrain. The plantation and the area
around it was a bad place to work, first because it was saturated with
Viet Cong and second because it was filled with civilians, most of
whom were sympathetic to the revolution. There were villages everywhere, and in the villages were children, women, old men—and
guerrillas. The rules of engagement were less precise than they are
now, but the general procedure was that if you were fired on, you
could fire back. This was not a problem with small arms. Where the
dilemma came was in deciding whether or not to use artillery and
air strikes—air and arty, in the vernacular—when, how much and
where. The matter was often argued among the men on off-duty
hours: You approach a village and receive rifle fire. You take casualties. You know that air and arty can wipe out the village. You also
know there are women and children in the village. What do you do?

There was no solid answer, and no rule in the book to go by.
Most infantry officers, if asked about it, would reply that their first
duty was the safety of the men under their command. To ensure
that safety most officers would take the village under artillery fire.
When the village was flattened, the men could move through it in
relative safety. The safety was still only relative because certainly
some snipers would be left. The Viet Cong knew the problems, and
often deliberately fired at troops from villages, or fired at planes
which flew too low over villages. The air or artillery barrage that
followed usually killed enough civilians to embitter the community
permanently against the Americans. Some American officers knew
this, and knew also that the disaffection of an entire community was

not worth the handful of Viet Cong that would be killed in a retaliation. So the argument was joined.

This was precisely the choice faced by a young battalion commander of the 1st Division one day that May. In the morning, two companies from the battalion were lifted by helicopter to a point just south of Thanh An village. The day before, the Vietnamese district chief asked that the village not be pre-struck with either air or artillery. The village was under the control of the Viet Cong, but the district chief assured the Americans that there were friendly people inside. There had been no intention to strike the village, but the American authorities noted the request.

This was before there was any trouble. The young battalion commander landed with the two companies and immediately ordered them to move out along a line of rubber trees toward the village. The first contact came when the point man of the lead squad spotted five Viet Cong preparing a booby trap. Shots were exchanged and the five men fled into the bush, in the direction of Thanh An village.

From another position to the north, still some distance from the village, the commander of the second company saw the flash of a mortar. He moved his lead squads to the fringes of the village, received machine-gun fire, and withdrew. There were several wounded. "We didn't get too far," the battalion commander said later. "We stopped and returned the fire."

All of this sounds precise and a little sterile, as if the action were taking place on a parade ground or in a city park. In fact the geography of the villages near the Michelin plantation made them very difficult to fight in. There were clearings surrounded by rain forests, and thick cover was everywhere. The village was not a neat entity, like a city block, but a scattered collection of wooden and straw huts, which meandered out from a common center. The land was flat and filled with brush, so progress was slow and uncertain. It was difficult to know exactly where you were. In the case of the battalion commander, whose name was Hathaway, there was great difficulty in locating the lead squads. The mortars and arty could reach into the village with impunity. But for men to move in and occupy the village was a tricky and intricate business; it was dangerous. The terrain favored the enemy, and so did the position of the village. From time to time the infantrymen saw women and children hurrying on the footpaths that laced the area; it was obvious that when they returned to Thanh An they would give the guerrillas a detailed explanation of the American positions, and weaponry.

And there was the heat. Each man carried three hundred rounds of ammunition, food, three filled canteens, a pack, his six-pound rifle, usually two or three hand grenades, and other amenities meant to make life in the jungle tolerable. But the heat reached 120 degrees in that jungle. The infantryman would begin to sweat in a steady stream and then, without warning, dry up. When he stopped sweating, he dropped from heat exhaustion, retching, brain burning up, semi-conscious. When it was hottest, large red soldier ants would drop off the trees and onto the neck and shoulders, where they would chew the flesh. It is an impossible way to fight, and commanders learned that a battalion could not be kept in the field more than four or five days at a time. Too many men would be lost to the heat.

Lt. Col. Ed Hathaway was faced with the question of bringing artillery to bear. If the village was a typical Viet Cong village, there would be reinforced bunkers made of concrete and wood under most of the houses. These were so carefully constructed that they could withstand anything but a direct hit. If the guerrillas followed true to form they would withdraw at the first sign of an artillery barrage. If the artillery pattern were well laid, there was a fair chance of killing a few as they withdrew. If an air strike were brought in, the chances were better than fair. There was no question that the village was controlled and dominated by the Viet

Cong. It was not a matter of bombing peasants who had pledged themselves to the Saigon government, or the Americans. Hathaway knew that peasants in that part of Vietnam, particularly the women and children and elderly men, rarely undertook conscious political commitment. To his conscience they were civilians. Hathaway thought about the artillery and then decided against it. The cost of life would be too great. He decided to meet the Viet Cong on its own terms.

His men advanced in the early morning, keeping low and moving steadily as they had been taught at the camps in the United States. They moved from house to hut down the narrow paths. They were hit from entrenched positions, as the guerrillas evacuated out the rear of the village, retreating before the Americans coming in the front. Viet Cong leaflets were scattered everywhere. There were slogans in English painted on the walls:

> Don't be a tool of the Wall Street warmongers. American Yankee imperialists go home.

The advancing Americans found a tailor shop for manufacturing enemy uniforms, and a cache of sixty-eight weapons. Hathaway's troops moved slowly and carefully through the village, firing as they went, the VC retreating just ahead of them. As the Americans passed the houses, women and children emerged from the tunnels beneath. There was a tunnel beneath each house. At midafternoon the village was cleared in a final skirmish. A dozen armed men were seen to move through the high grass near a stream, mingle with civilians, then disappear. Hathaway lost fifteen men to gunshot wounds. There were no civilian casualties. More important, from the viewpoint of the division general staff, there were no Viet Cong casualties. None. Not a single body was found. There was no evidence the guerrillas suffered a single wound.

The Americans were cut down as they advanced through the village. As they fell, medics applied morphine and helped them to the rear. Then medical evacuation helicopters flew them off to the field hospital. By dusk, the Americans had occupied the town of Thanh An.

It was just dusk when the assistant commander of the division, Brigadier General James H. Hollingsworth, arrived in his helicopter. Hollingsworth had heard of the fifteen wounded men and went immediately to Hathaway's command post. He was angry, and as he came out of the helicopter he had his helmet tucked under his arm and moved quickly and powerfully, swinging his arms like a college halfback. Captain Gerald Griffin, a veteran company commander, and now the operations officer of Hathaway's battalion, stood nearby, nervous and looking straight ahead. Hathaway and one of his staff majors watched Hollingsworth approach across the clearing.

There were a few pleasantries and then Hollingsworth asked how many men had been hit.

"The report isn't in, Sir," Hathaway said.

"I heard on the radio that it was fifteen, and maybe more," Hollingsworth said.

"Well, they weren't KIA. They were wounded," Hathaway said.

"It was about fifteen wounded. We're getting the complete count now," said Griffin.

"That's a lot of wounded. Any KIA at all?"

"No KIA."

The general asked the lieutenant colonel what had happened, and Hathaway told him the story. "I didn't fire the artillery into the town. There were hundreds of them in there. We counted more than two hundred women and children, and fifty elderly men. I guess there were about a squad of VC. Twenty, maybe thirty of the bastards."

Hollingsworth nodded and said nothing. He still had the steel helmet tucked under his arm, football-style. He was looking at the ground, the toe of his boot describing a small circle in the dust.

"It was my decision to make," Hathaway told him, "and I elected not to do it."

"Well, you took some wounded," Hollingsworth said.

"Yes, sir," Hathaway said.

"And didn't get any VC."

"No, sir. Maybe if I had it to do over again, I'd do it differently." Hathaway was a tall, handsome, career army officer from somewhere in Virginia. Before he had come to Vietnam he had been in charge of assignments. He once remarked that if he didn't want to be in Vietnam, he wouldn't have been. Now he was nervous and standing ramrod-straight before Hollingsworth.

The general patted Hathaway on the shoulder and made as if to go. He asked him if he had enough C rations and water for the night, and if ammunition was plentiful. The men in the clearing were digging in. The two officers stood for a minute saying nothing, looking out over the field and to the rain forest beyond. It was dark now and the battalion headquarters was battening down for the night. Hollingsworth grunted and said Jesus, he didn't know what he would have done in that situation. He thought that probably he would have brought in the arty, and the hell with the civilians. A military officer is responsible for his men in a war, and goddamnit it was a war. But it was a hell of a war. The general turned to Hathaway and patted him on the shoulder again and said he thought it was a decision no man should be forced to make. *No man should be forced to make that kind of choice.* What kind of enemy was it that hid behind women and children?

OF COURSE most of it was not like that at all. Most of it had no drama and no style, and no morals of any kind. The infantryman called it hard slogging or humping. One day became much like the next, a calendar checkmark closer to the day of departure from South Vietnam. The days stretched endlessly, like the paddies and the rain forests. It became then a matter of simply moving with care. It was like this when nothing was happening, but everybody was digging in.

The sun was descending and the sky turned the color of lead. The company command post had not moved all afternoon, had stayed in place while the company commander awaited instructions from battalion headquarters. Its patrols had found nothing. There were no Viet Cong anywhere.

But this was said to be a Communist base area, this slice of jungle west of the special forces camp at Sui Da, a forty-five-minute helicopter ride north and west of Saigon. The company commander ordered the mortars out and registered. There were three mortars and each was zeroed in on half a dozen different targets around the company's perimeter. There were thirty minutes of firing the mortars, the explosions marking a circle around the command post.

If your eyes are good you can see the mortar shell as it leaves the tube, arcs very high in the air, and falls. These mortar shells were falling very close to the perimeter. The men ducked when they fell, and hurried to finish digging foxholes. The company commander, a captain of infantry, put the scouts out, and the two ambush patrols, the flares, and the other paraphernalia of living for a night in War Zone C, Tay Ninh province.

This was part of operation Attleboro, which in November and December, 1966, occupied the better part of two American divisions. The objective was to sweep and clear, search and destroy, Viet Cong base areas in Tay Ninh and Binh Duong. The terrain was flat and thick with jungle. Intelligence reports were vague. Companies would maneuver for days, and never see the enemy. Then without warning they would stumble into a base camp and fight for two days. War Zone C, any part of it, is known as a Viet Cong sanctuary, but that is, or was, about all that was known. The companies were expected to sweep until they ran into something. When they ran into something, they fought it.

There was artillery from Sui Da, eight miles to the east, and this was called in "for effect," as the soldier says, to make certain that coordinates on the map were exact, that if the company's position were attacked that night the shells could be fired immediately and precisely around the perimeter. The artillery was meant to back up the mortar fire. This was standard defense against enemy infiltration at night. It was before the Viet Cong had acquired so many mortars of their own; the only real defense against mortars are deep holes.

"If there are a hell of a lot of Cong," the CO told his platoon leaders, "don't fire."

The men were standing in the darkness, cupping their cigarettes.

"Lay low, and don't for God's sake withdraw. I don't want to see anybody shot in the darkness."

"Have you people all got a compass?"

The others fished around in their jackets. They all had compasses.

"When you see them ahead of you," the CO went on, "you have got to give me the azimuth. You have got to say how many there are, and how many meters they are in front of you. And you *have got* to give me the azimuth. If I don't have the azimuth I can't bring in either the mortars or the artillery."

The CO turned to each man to make certain the instructions were clear and understood, and each man knew where to go. There was some confusion over that, so the map was brought out again. The CO was new to Vietnam. It was his first combat command, and the first patrol for many of his men, draftees newly disembarked from air force jets at Tan Son Nhut. He didn't want a bitched job.

When the artillery was called in "for effect" one of the infantry-men on the perimeter stood up and caught a shell fragment in the belly. For a moment or two everyone thought he was dead, but it was only a superficial wound. A few of the men laughed, and the CO exploded: "God-damnit shut up and get back to the line." A helicopter was summoned and the injured man evacuated.

At seven o'clock, deep dusk in the jungle, a rifleman burst into the command post. He had seen a Viet Cong prowling the perimeter. The VC had tried to fire his weapon, but it had jammed. Then he vanished. The CO and the others assumed it was a probe prior to an attack. It was certain now that the company would be hit. Then suddenly a chatter of rifle fire erupted behind the CP and everyone went flat. The CO and two lieutenants and the sergeant in the CP went for the field telephones and within minutes artillery rounds were whistling overhead. The sergeant was on the line to the man who fired. It was fifteen minutes before they sorted it out, but the man who fired was shooting at another American manning a listening post farther forward: the artillery was called off. The CO sent out new instructions to be careful and certain before firing weapons.

"We'll never know how many screw-ups they have," the CO said to his operations officer.

"I suppose as many as we do."

"More, probably," said the CO.

"They don't have our communications."

"Shit, that's a blessing."

"Well, there aren't any of those newspaper people with *them*. They screw up, and nobody reads about it."

"It'd be goddamned nice if everything would go right, for once," the CO said.

"You bet," said his operations officer.

It began to rain. The infantryman sits in his hole, cupping a cigarette and trying to keep the water off his face. The lucky ones were at the CP, where reinforced bunkers had been dug (probably by the Viet Cong a year or so before). Some of the men slept in the bunkers, others made a tent from the heavy rubber poncho, regular army issue, that soldiers carry. You put the tent up, then dug an inch-deep trench around the tent. The trench supposedly caught the water that came off the tent. An infantryman learned to make himself as comfortable as possible.

Then at midnight one of the men in a forward listening post thought he heard someone, probably a Communist, cough. So artillery was brought in for half an hour. Then one of the men thought he heard someone, presumably a Communist, move through the jungle. Artillery was brought in again. One of the sergeants was unimpressed. "A shee-it," he said. "They're shooting at deer, probably."

"If you've gotta be one," said a droll Southern gunny from his hole nearby, "better be a big red one." It was a reference to the outfit, the 1st Infantry Division, sometimes known as the Big Red One. Except it was spoken, Big Red *One,* with the accent on the last word. The CO smiled sourly.

There were urgent conferences in the command post, with the CO and his aides bent over maps plotting the enemy's location. The dim red glow of the flashlights was just visible from ten yards away. The men were whispering into the field telephone, trying to get precise angles—the azimuth—from the men in the line. The artillery boomed and the exploding shells shook the earth, sending shock waves through the CP. The company's mortars were fired several times. When one of the men stood up to get a better look at the blast, he caught a mortar fragment under the eye. But in the darkness, no medical evacuation helicopter could land. The injury was not serious enough for evacuation anyway.

The infantryman tries to sleep with the artillery blowing up one part of the jungle, and mortars tearing hell out of the other part, and the company commander and his lieutenants talking into the field telephone and worrying about whether they would have to face a large-scale attack. There was some talk of bugles and a human wave assault, and the proper tactics if they were surrounded. The men on the perimeter were reporting back every few minutes and the CO grew increasingly nervous. But the infantryman, lying there in the rain, could think of home or the fact that Christmas was two weeks away. He could reflect that six hours before the paymaster had been through, setting down smartly in a D-model Huey helicopter, distributing the funny money, the military-issue scrip with which you could buy a Sony tape recorder or a bottle of Seagram's 7 Crown in the PX, if you could get to the PX. The money came in a large black bag. And the mail had come (the CO himself had two unread letters from his wife in the breast pockets of his fatigues). The company had had A rations—a hot meal of roast beef and mashed potatoes and boiled carrots flown in from division headquarters at Dau Tieng. But it was a long night, and the officers bent over their maps and tried to devise a strategy against an enemy which attacked without warning.

There were no bugles or human wave assaults, nor so much as a sniper round. There was silence between two and five A.M. and the men in the command post slept then. The rain stopped and the stars came out, along with the crickets and jungle leeches. It was very cool in the jungle at night.

Forward elements of the company moved out before nine. The command group waited until just after noon, then it moved out too. The command group picked its way along a trail that wound through the jungle in the direction of Cambodia. On either side were deep slit trenches. The trenches contained rusty tins of C rations, and Diet Cola and Hamm's Beer, the legacy of the last time the Americans had swept and cleared that part of War Zone C.

IT WAS not all post-mortem, or boredom, or aimless conversation, either. Occasionally you would see a confrontation so stark and brutal that it illuminated everything, and told you as much about the war as you wanted to know. Or, really, it didn't tell you anything about the war in Vietnam. It told you a certain amount about some of the men who fought it. It came as a surprise that there were men who wanted to fight it, and not necessarily for reasons of repressed violence. There were killers in Vietnam, as there are in Chicago or Singapore, and they liked Vietnam for the blood. But there were others who liked it for other reasons.

The company commander was dead, shot through the forehead, and was lying somewhere down the hill. One of his radio operators was dead, and so was a rifleman. Six more were wounded, and a sergeant was missing. Now the company had pulled back from the firing and was scrambling up the hill.

The hill and the jungle surrounding it was nameless, a trackless uninhabited forest about a mile from the Cambodian border, south of the Ia Drang Valley, west and south of Pleiku. There was a battalion of the 1st Cavalry Division in place north of the hill. Two companies had been sent out that morning on probing missions. Intelligence had placed two battalions, perhaps a regiment, of Viet Cong or North Vietnamese in the area. The Americans were there to try to entrap the enemy and make him stick and fight. The cavalry had units strung along the border trying to find both the Viet Cong and the North Vietnamese units crossing the Cambodian border.

What had happened that afternoon was a typically confusing "envelopment," as the strategists liked to call it. One company had moved out and was hit from ambush. But the attackers had made a mess of it, and only two Americans were wounded; they counterattacked, driving the enemy to the south. A second American company was moved into a blocking position, still farther to the south. The hope was that the first company would drive the retreating Viet Cong into the second company, and thus catch them as in a vise. The second company, Company C, was brought in by helicopter and as it moved out it was attacked, whether by the fleeing Viet Cong or by another enemy force was not known.

They were hit from three sides. The point man, or lead scout, went down wounded. The company commander scrambled to a spot near the wounded man to personally direct efforts to evacuate him back to the rear lines. The point man, hit badly and losing blood, was in an impossible position, under fire and away from the main American force. The captain, ignoring every rule including the simplest and most fundamental, moved to a position only slightly more tenable. He was shot in the head and died instantly. Then his radioman was hit.

The rest of the company, under fire from automatic weapons, began to withdraw up the hill to the high ground. The high ground was held by the rear American elements and technically should have been secure, but it was not. There was sniper fire all over the hill, and it was impossible to tell where it was coming from. So the harassing fire continued and the men withdrew up the hill. There were not many wounded and even fewer dead, but the men were exhausted and confused as they moved through the trees up the hill. The captain was left where he fell. So were the two others who were killed, and so was a platoon sergeant. The sergeant had got separated and no one knew whether he was dead or alive; he was presumed to be dead. Some thought he was still alive and game, and waiting for a chance to break free and get up the hill.

The Cuban was waiting for the forward squads as they came slowly through the trees. Everyone was drawn and weary except for the Cuban, who walked upright with indifference and contempt for the enemy fire. He was standing next to a tree, expressionless and gripping an M–16 rifle, when a very young, light-haired lieutenant walked over and gripped him by the arm.

"Look, I'm sorry," the lieutenant said. The sergeant didn't say anything, and the lieutenant went on. "We couldn't do it. I was ten feet behind him and I couldn't do it. Bullets were everywhere. I couldn't do it."

"Ten feet? You were ten feet away?" The Cuban sergeant was incredulous.

"It was a long ten feet. The bullets were nicking the tree and that was how we could tell where the shooting was coming from, the angles of the trajectory of the bullets as they hit the tree." He used his hands, in a downward slashing motion. "The only way we could have gotten to the captain was by walking into the bullets."

"Yeah," said the Cuban, drawing the word out, Yeaahhh.

"Geez, you should have seen the fire. Hairy, my God, it was so hairy; it was the worst I've ever seen it. Geez, it was hairy." The lieutenant was pleading.

"So the captain is still there?"

"We couldn't do it, I tell you," said the lieutenant. "There's no good adding dead to dead."

The Cuban shook his head.

"More dead. It would have meant five more dead to get the old man out of there." The lieutenant laughed nervously. "You wouldn't have believed how much fire there was." He pointed to a cut on his cheek. "One of the bullets nicked a tree or something and a fragment got me there."

But the Cuban sergeant wasn't looking at the lieutenant's cheek. He was looking into his blue eyes. "The old man was a hell of a man," said the Cuban. Then, in one of those phrases out of an army citation, "He was a hell of a fine, aggressive officer."

The Cuban looked at the lieutenant for a minute, then walked away about twenty yards and began poking the end of his rifle butt into the ground. He had been at the rear end of the column, away from the heaviest fire and away from the captain. But he had heard that the captain had gone to help the wounded point man. His face was still expressionless as he poked the rifle butt into the ground.

The young lieutenant walked over to his platoon and sat down heavily, shaking his head and worrying. "Christ, I fucked up," he said. "Christ, I really fucked up."

The executive officer, who had assumed command when the CO was hit, was talking into the telephone, arranging for an air strike and trying to figure out how to get the bodies back. The wounded were all right. He said that the CO was surely dead, but there was a platoon sergeant at the bottom of the hill whom nobody knew about. No one knew whether he was dead or alive, or what. But the air strike was necessary. The executive officer estimated that his company had been hit by at least a company of North Vietnamese, who were still in the gully. There was a good chance that an air strike would clear them out.

The Cuban had been listening to all of this. He was a refugee from Castro who said he understood what the Vietnam war was all about. He had volunteered for it and wanted to fight it. The most important thing in the world was that America stop Communism in Asia. He said his parents were dead because of Castro and Castro's revolution, and if the United States stood firm in Southeast Asia Communism could be stopped. It was either there or in Hawaii. He said that he had been part of the landing force at the Bay of Pigs, but did not go beyond that. The point was that he knew what he was doing in Vietnam; that was for damned sure.

The young lieutenant, now daubing at the cut on his cheek, walked over again to explain about the captain. He carried a copy of *Time* magazine in his trousers pocket, and worried about his wife. He hoped she would not hear about what happened today, the fuck-up.

"Look," he said to the Cuban, "you understand what it was like down there."

"Yeah," said the Cuban, and walked off.

The bombing began and the harassing Viet Cong fire ended. The wounded were at the crest of the hill, waiting for evacuation. The bombs from the American planes were still falling, hitting so close to the hilltop that small fragments hit the trees and the rocks. The men stayed crouched down, eyes to the earth. At twenty yards away the Cuban stood alone, clearing his rifle, waiting for the bombardment to end. When it did he took his rifle and three volunteers and went down into the gully to reclaim the body of the company commander.

Somewhere in all of that I thought there was a fine novel. Hiep, Hathaway and Hollingsworth, the Cuban and the lieutenant, were all good novel people, and so was the sarcastic sergeant who talked about what a fine thing, a *good* thing, it was to be a "big red *one.*" There was a book as good as *A Farewell to Arms* in the stories, if you had the wit to see it and the imagination to generalize from it. But it never worked out that way, and one was left with another fragment, another note toward the definition of the Vietnam war. One hoped that it would be useful, writing about the kid who quit in the middle of a fight, or the casual murder of a Vietnamese café owner in Binh Dinh province (by a half-dozen drunk Ruff-Puffs), the American provincial representative in the Delta whose sister lived in the Congo and collected the effects of dead Belgian mercenaries, the poor boy named Truman Shockley who was shot through the heart by a sniper one afternoon just as he lit a Lucky Strike cigarette. I used Shockley four different ways in four different stories, to make four different points. But it was only a fragment. I didn't have any more to go on than his name, and the memory of the shots and his falling, and the attempts to revive him.

6

RECONNAISSANCE

IN THE SUMMER of 1966 yet another monsoon offensive was predicted in Pleiku and Kontum provinces in the Central Highlands. American intelligence said the North Vietnamese were infiltrating from Laos into Pleiku and Kontum in battalion- and regimental-sized units, well fed, well trained and well and heavily armed. The theory of the enemy objective, which had been expounded in one form or another for two years, was that Giap's regulars would "cut the country in half," driving east from the Laotian border to the South China Sea. It was an implausible theory, owing as it did practically nothing to logic: the North Vietnamese did not have the men to hold a line across the waist of South Vietnam, neither did they have the weapons to ward off attacking American aircraft. Much more plausible was the theory that the North Vietnamese were invading to make the highlands so hazardous that the Americans would be forced to concentrate large numbers of troops there.

But everybody believed the scissors theory, probably because it made rich newspaper copy. An American general once admitted that what the command had in mind was that if the North Vietnamese cut the country in half they would have a marvelous propaganda victory. The reverse was also true, and therein lay the *raison d'être* for the theory. The operative line was given at a Westmoreland press briefing in 1966: "They tried to cut the country in half but we stopped them."

There were a few amateur strategists who insisted that the country was already cut in half, obviously so by the inability of an ordinary citizen to drive from Saigon to the Demilitarized Zone. But these objections were swept aside as the work of cranks. As far as the American command was concerned, the North Vietnamese went on trying to cut the country in half and the American Army went on stopping them. Thus was the territorial integrity of South Vietnam preserved.

No one knew what the strategy really was. Some of the military thinkers believed that all Ho and Giap had in mind was sending as many troops as they could afford, punishing the Americans to the limit of endurance, and assaulting airfields and base camps until the allies quit from exhaustion. It was, as Westmoreland often said in 1967, a war of attrition; grand strategy did not as a practical matter exist. It was tactics that counted, and what was meant by tactics were the thousands of small-unit engagements from the Camau peninsula to the DMZ. The sum of these equaled the whole, or should have.

I flew from Saigon to Pleiku and then to the Special Forces camp at Dak To early in June, 1966. I had been told in Saigon that American intelligence officers had identified new North Vietnamese units prowling the highlands. The 1st Brigade of the 101st Airborne Division was to move out into the jungles to find the enemy. It was regarded in Saigon as an important campaign: whatever the argument on whether or not the enemy objective was to cut the country in half, there was no doubt that the highlands themselves were imperiled.

It was the North Vietnamese who drew first blood: on the night of June 6, a battalion hit an American artillery base just north of Dak To and nearly overran it. Firing at point-blank range, the Americans had managed to beat back the attack. Following normal procedure, enemy troops had carried their dead from the battle-field. Only two bodies were left behind, but the artillerymen were confident many, many more had died. No one knew how many. What was surprising was the closeness of the engagement. "You could see the enemy," said one young artillery captain, in wonder. "They saw us and we saw them." It didn't happen that way very often, which lent an interesting and appealing tone to the opening engagement of the operation which would be called Hawthorne, or the campaign for the control of the Central Highlands.

The commander of the 1st Battalion, 327th Infantry of the 101st Airborne Brigade, Major David Hackworth, was standing amid the ruins of the camp when I alighted from a helicopter in the company of one of the ubiquitous public relations men of the American Army. We had been flying for nearly an hour, trying to find the base which was neatly hidden in the crotch of two hills. It had been an unnerving ride, since the hills were nominally, or more than nomi-nally, enemy territory. Hackworth briefly explained the situation, then said with a grin that he was sending one of the reconnaissance units ("recondo," in Airborne argot, meaning commando/recon-naissance) deep into the mountains to find the enemy base camp, and to try in the process to round up enemy stragglers. Hackworth was so cheerful about the prospect of heading into the mountains that I instantly asked to go along. He said fine, then introduced me to Captain Lewis Higinbotham, the commander of the 42-man Tiger Force, as the recondo platoon was known. "You'll like Higinbotham," Hackworth said. "He's a good killer."

Hackworth had words for the men of the Tiger Force, who were now assembling their weapons and gear, and the words went like this: "Goddamnit I want forty hard-charging fuckin' dicks. And if anybody ain't a hard-charging fuckin' dick I want him out."

"Fuckin'," muttered one of the men.

"Right," said Hackworth.

"Fuckin'," the trooper muttered again.

The English language, like everything else in Vietnam, became unreal after a time. Hackworth's words were—words. He might have appealed for forty soft-bellied capons, or forty fine, aggressive young American soldiers, or forty draft-dodgers, or forty journalists, or forty fat congressmen from Texas. As it was, he appealed for forty hard-charging fuckin' dicks. It didn't matter. I unconsciously wrote the words in my notebook.

Then Hackworth turned to me, banging the palms of his hands together. Matters were looking up. "My God, we chased them for five days over every flipping hill in Vietnam. Five days! And they hit us back here. They kept one hill ahead of us. One hill all along the way. Well, now they've had it."

The Airborne had that reputation.

A unit assembles its reputation from many sources, but mainly from its commanders. These were the commanding general, Brigadier General Willard Pearson, and the two battalion commanders, Lt. Colonel Henry Emerson, and Major Hackworth. There were others, but these were the principal ones. They were professional soldiers, none more so than Pearson, who was the architect of the Brigade's bold and successful jungle tactics. Briefly, these were to probe as far into enemy territory as possible, make contact, then reinforce by helicopter. It required using small units as bait, which you could do only if your men were anxious to fight, and had proved it by signing on as paratroopers, for more money and prestige in the services. Pearson's reputation as a soldier was excellent, but he had strange lapses when dealing with men. Once, approaching a particularly difficult mission, he promised a company of infantry a case of beer if the mission were successful. In those circles, a case of beer was regarded as barely adequate for one man, let alone 200. Pearson, the strategist who wanted to carry the war to the enemy on the enemy's terms, was regarded with a mixture of respect and astonishment.

Not so Hackworth and Emerson. They were quite simply admired, as men and as soldiers. Personal courage is a very attractive quality in men. It is the one quality, as someone said, which guarantees all the others. Hackworth had it, and so did Emerson. They were brave men, without being excessively reckless or self-conscious about it. Hackworth was especially appealing. He seemed to be amused at the whole apparatus of the war in Vietnam; he knew that things were never what they seemed, and that you kept your sanity only by admitting a whole range of possibilities. That day, in the center of the artillery fire base, he strode around with a tiny riding crop, disheveled, unshaven and profane, and after a bit took Higinbotham aside to brief him on the mission.

Lew Higinbotham looked an unlikely killer. Slim, bony-faced, Texas-accented, he was polite and grim, and the dirt deliberately smeared over his cheeks and chin did not conceal youth. He was in his middle twenties, unmarried, a career soldier. Higinbotham had been in Vietnam more than two years, most of it spent in the Delta south of Saigon as an adviser to Vietnamese troops. This was his first mission with the Tiger Force. It was an elite unit and Higinbotham was anxious to do well; he liked the Vietnamese, but preferred to work with Americans. The forty-two men under his command were a rugged and motley lot, bringing to mind one of those posses assembled from the worst saloons on Main Street in the Grade B horse operas. Unshaven, dirty, unlettered, mean, nervous; one was in flight from his third wife, another (so the story went) from the police, a third was in Vietnam because he liked to kill Charlie Cong. Some of the others had the spirit of buccaneers, fugitives from a safe society. They liked the adventure, and the weapons. One of them regularly sent the ears of dead Viet Cong to his wife, through the army postal system. Half the platoon was Negro. One of these, informed that a journalist would be along on the patrol, became helpless with laughter. He doubled up, face shaking with mirth at the madness of it all. "Sheet," he said. "Shee-it."

While the men got their gear together, checked weapons and gathered up food and ammunition, I prowled around the edges of the artillery base. There were dark streaks of blood where men had been carried off the night before. Part of a torso lay just beyond the security perimeter. On the top of a small rise I looked north, and saw high hills without signs of life. There were no villages in this part of Kontum. There were some Montagnard tribesmen, but nothing else. In the old days of the French occupation, the hills were often used for tiger hunts. We loaded into helicopters and were off.

The land north of Dak To was rugged and uneven, high hills and thick jungle laced with trails. It was cool as we were dropped at four o'clock in the afternoon in a high stand of elephant grass. The trees had two growths of branches, one about six feet up the trunk and the other about twelve feet. They blotted out the sun. The light appeared to come through a great green-glass bottle without rays or beams. Higinbotham and I moved beneath one of the trees, and waited until the rest of the forty-two were accounted for. There was another captain there, and Higinbotham introduced him as Christ Verlumis, a 27-year-old career man from Oakland, California. Verlumis was the commander of headquarters company, to which the Tiger Force was technically attached. It was Verlumis's first week in Vietnam, and his first patrol. Higinbotham was not happy about the arrangement, because Verlumis technically outranked him—or was, in any case, in command of a larger unit. If there was trouble, and there was bound to be trouble, Higinbotham did not want to have to worry about another captain. And he didn't want to be second-guessed. Higinbotham had told all this to Hackworth. But Verlumis wanted to come, and so Verlumis came.

We moved out along a trail north and west roughly in the direction of the Laos border. Right away we fell upon a two-man position carved into a bush. It was deserted. The trail was well-traveled, and almost immediately there was another small hut ("hootch," to American soldiers in Vietnam) and then a third. Then, as we wound up the trail, there was a small base camp, perhaps large enough to accommodate a squad of a dozen men. In Vietnam action usually comes without warning. All of these installations on the trail were signs, warning signals that enemy troops were there. Higinbotham knew it and the men knew it. I knew it.

We were moving quickly, winding up the trail as the light faded and noting all the signs of enemy occupation. Then there was a burst of machine-gun fire, a shout, and all of the men flopped, and scurried off the trail into the shelter of the trees and bushes. The firing had come from the rear of the column, three fast bursts and now it was silent. Higinbotham urgently radioed his rear squad. One enemy soldier was dead, but one of our own men was hurt.

Private First Class Richard Garcia was lying off the trail, blood leaking from a wound in his chest. Three men stood over him, while the medic punctured his arm with a morphine needle. The men moved their feet and talked quietly to Garcia, although he was nearly unconscious. He had been hit by one of our own bullets; it is difficult to see in the jungle. No one knows where the enemy is, and the frightened man sprays with his weapon. He fires it in bursts, and none too accurately. One of these had caught Garcia in the lung. The medic was working frantically, muttering and cursing under his breath. Suddenly Garcia sat up, and looked straight at the medic: "I can't breathe. I am going home. I am going to be OK." Then he was dead.

Fifty yards away, the men of the rear squad were looking after the dead Vietnamese. He had been shot in the chest, but that was only the most recent wound. His head had been bandaged, and so had his leg. Higinbotham, looking at the body, decided he had been on his way back to the base camp for medical attention. He was probably one of those wounded in the attack on the artillery fire base the night before. Next to the body lay a battered, damaged AK–47 submachine gun. That was the standard weapon of the North Vietnamese Army, Soviet-designed and manufactured in China.

Higinbotham reported both deaths to battalion headquarters. "We've got a KIA, one of theirs and one of ours," Higinbotham said. The G–2 (intelligence officer) on the other end of the line warned him to be on the watch for more enemy. "Maybe a battalion more," the G–2 said.

The light was going, almost visibly as lights dim in a theater, and Higinbotham decided to stay where he was for the night. Garcia's body was taken down to the trail and three men prepared it for transport on a litter. His arms were folded on his chest, and his blouse pulled up tight over his face and head. Then the body, compact in the camouflaged uniform, hatless, was tied to the litter, and the pack was tied to the body; lying there that night Garcia looked comfortable. Higinbotham said it was possible he was killed by rifle fire from the Vietnamese, but most likely not; most likely he was killed from our own lines. It was a matter of fire discipline, Higinbotham said; there was never enough of it, and too many people were killed needlessly. But you couldn't prevent all of it. With all the lead flying around, people got hurt; it was not a factor you could control.

The men arranged themselves in a star-shaped defense, three to a group. One man in each group stayed awake at all times. There would be no talking or smoking and the radio would be off. The jungle in Kontum goes dark before seven. The wetness comes as it grows black, and except for the chattering of the small birds and animals it is silent; after a while the bird and animal sounds become part of the silence. Because of the rot which turns the plants to phosphorus, the jungle floor is brilliant with light, enough light to see your fingernail or read the dials on a wristwatch. I had a small flask of whiskey, which I passed to Higinbotham and Verlumis and the radio operator, Terry Grey. We talked quietly of one thing and another, colleges, life on the West Coast, and then tried to sleep. I recalled a line from A. J. Liebling that when he was in an uncomfortable or dangerous spot during World War II, and he was trying to sleep, he thought about women. It seemed a sensible and distracting idea, so from nine that night until seven the next morning I thought about women.

We awoke slowly and crawled quietly from beneath the bushes to stretch as daylight came. With it came the second omen. There was a shout, a rattle of gunfire, and we were all on our bellies in that awful initial confusion. Suddenly a sheepish private stood before Higinbotham. There were three armed Vietnamese, uniformed and not alert, the private said. They stumbled into camp, saw the Americans, and fled. The GI's, equally startled, had time for only a half-dozen rounds. The three enemy soldiers scampered across a small stream and disappeared into the bush. Higinbotham shook his head, and smiled. "Oh hell, they probably spent the night with us," he said. "They probably thought we were the 226th North Vietnamese Regiment, for crissakes." Higinbotham reported the incident to G–2, which received the information without comment.

A long-range reconnaissance patrol cannot operate once its presence is known to the enemy. Twice the Tigers had been forced to fire. Now three Vietnamese had seen them, and had escaped, and were certainly bound for their headquarters. None of this could have been foreseen, and there was nothing to be done about it. But it was terrible luck. Security, to the extent that there was any in the middle of a jungle in the middle of enemy territory, was compromised. It had to be considered compromised, although the mission itself was not in doubt. The mission went on. There was no place to go but forward, deeper and higher into the hills, discovering enemy base camps and rounding up stragglers. The patrol was still well within the range of the brigade's artillery, and the operations officer was keeping careful check on our precise location. Word has been fed back that the enemy was known to be operating in the area; but Higinbotham knew that.

The objective now was to find a landing zone for a helicopter to come in and "extract" Garcia. Garcia was a burden and there was no room now for burdens. "I don't like any part of it," Higinbotham said.

Kontum that day was marvelously cool, and we crossed half a dozen small streams on our way up the hill. There was no movement except for an occasional exquisitely colored butterfly. The men moved very quietly and carefully. A clearing was found, and Garcia lifted out; the helicopter crew left a dozen cases of C rations behind. The men dug into the cases labeled, in the weird army phraseology, MEAL, COMBAT, INDIVIDUAL—like that, with commas. They were looking for cigarette packages and fruit. Each meal carton contained a little package of condiments: salt, pepper, sugar, powdered cream, coffee, gum, toilet paper, matches, and a package of five cigarettes; the brands were Camels, Chesterfields, Salems, Newports, Winstons, or Pall Malls. At least two of the large cases were untouched, so a hole was dug and they were buried. We moved out again.

The trail meandered into deeper jungle, with base camp following base camp. Higinbotham decided by one in the afternoon that his band had uncovered a staging area capable of accommodating a regiment of 1,000 men. The knowledge was not comforting. The men, in soft hats, their faces smeared with mud, carefully cradling weapons, kept silently climbing, turning their eyes off the trail and into the bush.

In two years in the Delta, Higinbotham had acquired a passable knowledge of Vietnamese. When his lead squad found a small arrow-shaped sign with the words *Anh Ban Di Trang,* he knew we were on the right trail, the pigeons among the cats. The words translated, "friends go straight"; it was obviously an enemy message. And with the Vietnamese talent for confusion, at the point of the sign the trail forked, with no clear indication which trail was meant. One branch led upward, along the small stream. The other moved left, down the hill. At the fork there were two huts where the command group waited: Higinbotham sent patrols down each trail. The first, led by Sergeant Pellum Bryant, almost immediately saw three enemy soldiers in the khaki uniforms of the North Vietnamese Army. Bryant opened fire with his M–16, and began heaving grenades. Everyone in the command post was flat on his stomach, waiting. The firing went on for five minutes, then ceased and Bryant returned to Higinbotham. He had got one, but the others had fled. Now from the other trail the radio crackled that there was resistance, that one Tiger was seriously wounded and the others pinned down.

Strung out in a long, thin line, the men moved down the trail and up to the ridge line. The patrol that had been hit was on the other side of the hill, which was not sharp but rolling, covered by deep jungle and ending in a steep ravine. At the top of the hill the men shed their packs, and a six-man patrol headed downslope to learn the American casualties and assess the strength of the enemy. It was impossible to judge distances because of the thickness of the cover.

The patrol reported back that the enemy had moved out; there was no more firing. Higinbotham nodded and, leaving six men behind to guard the rear, began to move down the trail to the ravine. It was a two-foot-wide trail that wound down and into a tiny cleft between the two hills. It then curled up the next hill. Edgy, edgy enough that a man snarled if you stumbled and stepped on his heel, the platoon moved down. There was a wounded GI in the crotch of the hills. He had been shot through the neck beside a cache of enemy rockets and grenades. The grenades were in a cave, carefully covered with tarpaulin. Four men went down to get the wounded man, crawling past the body of an enemy soldier whose head had been blown off in the firing ten minutes before. The wounded man was hurting, and scared. The hill was very steep, and the four found it difficult to slide down.

"You don't feel no pain, baby," the medic said, putting a needle into the man's arm. "You gonna be all right, baby. You gonna see that girl." The talk was all nonsense, meant to distract. The medic was wrapping a bandage around his comrade's neck. Another medic put a plasma needle into his right arm. The man's shirt was soaked with blood from the wound.

"I knew it," the wounded man said. "I knew that my chip was cashed in."

"We gonna get the MedEvac," the medic said.

"Well, that pilot better be there when I get there." Then, "You think I got a Stateside wound?"

The medic was worrying about the stretcher.

"Litter?"

"Litter!"

"Bring the litter, goddamnit."

"I wonder why my stomach hurts so much."

"Don't worry. This happens to everybody."

The wounded man, Private First Class Frank Wills, was at the base of a 45-degree incline. But the litter was there now, and the four men struggled and worried him up to the trail which led down from the ridge line.

It was very quiet, and no movement from anything. There were no birds or animals or butterflies, and the men were still and silent. Wills had become half-delirious from pain and fear. He asked again why his stomach hurt so much. Then he told the medic he had one hundred dollars in his pocket. "Take it and hold it for me," he said. Wills was thinking about going back home to Miami.

But the medic wasn't listening. No one was. Higinbotham was worried about Wills and whether a landing zone could be carved out of the hillside. It couldn't, and Higinbotham knew that. He also knew that his patrol was deep inside enemy lines with no way to get out, except to walk out. The patrol had found what it had come to find; the problem was what to do with it now. Enemy troops were obviously all around, and they knew that the Americans were there. Higinbotham squatted on the trail and wondered what to do.

The trail wound down from the ridge line perhaps one hundred yards. There were foxholes and bunkers all along it. Six men were at the top, guarding the packs, six more at the base. Higinbotham, Verlumis, Wills, the radio operator, Terry Grey; and twenty-five regulars were strung out along about fifty yards of the trail. There were plenty of grenades and plenty of ammunition. But Higinbotham thought about the deployment, and shuddered. They were not enough, not nearly enough if the enemy attacked from the ridge line; and the assumption had to be that that was what they would do.

"Hey, Mr. Reporter!" It was the trooper who found my presence so mirth-provoking. He began to laugh again, and so did I. It was an absurd predicament.

"You picked a great patrol," Higinbotham said.

"Mr. Reporter, how much you get paid for this?" the trooper asked.

"Not enough," I said.

"Damn," Higinbotham said, looking again at his maps.

Higinbotham's worries were not mine. Since the death of Garcia the night before, I had tried to concentrate on journalism. I had worked at taking careful notes and photographs, and now reflected on the similarity of the soldier and the war correspondent, the basic text for which comes from Joseph Heller's novel, *Catch–22*. On the one hand, no one wants to get ambushed or to be where bullets are fired in anger. On the other, if nothing happens there is no story. If the patrol does not meet the enemy, there is nothing to write about. It becomes a pointless exercise, a long walk under a hot sun. If the patrol does meet the enemy you are likely to be killed or wounded, or at the very least scared to death. *Catch–23.*

It was a bad catch. I worked at disbelief. You switch off, and pull all the plugs, severing connections. Your movements become slow and deliberate, and your consciousness seems to move back in time. The point is to maintain control. With forty-one men in the middle of a clearing in the middle of Kontum in the middle of a war, you are standing—nowhere. For distraction, think about women or squat down and pick blades of grass, chew them and put a film in the camera. Focus the lens. Make pictures of the American infantry. Transcribe dialogue:

"Sheet, I wrote her back she do anything she want."

"Well, we over here and they're there."

"Fuck that noise."

"Yeah."

"You hear Tomkins get killed?"

"Yeah?"

"Sheet, a mine blew him up and there was nuthin' left but nuthin'."

"Sheet."

"I tell you, Man, this is some kind of war."

"Sumthin' else!"

"Crise, I was in a platoon and there's nuthin' left of that platoon now. I'm the only one left."

"Gimme some fruit."

"Trayja fruit for some butts."

"Fuck you."

"Three butts."

"Whyn't you pick up the butts back there when we got 'em?"

"'Cause I was on point savin' your ass in case old Charlie come along."

"Gimme the fuckin' fruit."

"Three butts."

"Sheet, man, I ain't got but half a pack."

"Goddamn I got to get this weapon *fixed*."

"Hey, Mr. Reporter. What the fuck you doing here?"

At two-thirty in the afternoon the first grenade crashed down the ridge line. It went wide with a *thump*. Then *thump! Thumpthump!* Again, closer.

In the first fifteen minutes, three died and six fell wounded. The firing came from three sides, hitting the Americans at all points on the trail. The men guarding the packs at the top of the trail scattered under a hail of machine-gun fire. Only a few actually saw the enemy, who were maneuvering and firing as they maneuvered. Higinbotham at his command post halfway down the line knew the danger of the situation better than anybody else. He collected the first reports from his sergeants. The reports were only that there were a lot of enemy, and it was impossible to tell how many. Higinbotham called Hackworth at battalion headquarters and requested artillery fire and air support. It would come in the next four hours, 1,100 rounds of .105 and 90 rounds of .155 artillery. There would be air strikes, and the noise would be as if the world were coming apart.

No one knew then and no one knows now how many North Vietnamese there were. They did not have mortars, so the unit was probably company-sized or smaller. But they had grenades and small arms and automatic weapons, and good cover to shoot from. They fought from concealed positions and they had the element of surprise and knowledge of the terrain. It was, after all, their base camp.

American artillery shells fell in a wide semicircle just beyond the American positions. They were hitting at the ridge line and beyond, but the Vietnamese fire did not lessen. The planes attacked with a roar and without warning; because of the heavy cover they could not be seen. One fist-sized piece of shrapnel landed two feet from Higinbotham, but he did not cease talking into the field phone, precisely locating the positions of heaviest enemy fire. While the shells were landing, Americans were dying; a half dozen in the first half hour, another six in the five succeeding hours of combat.

In the command post, enemy rifle fire was hitting five feet high. We were all down, scanning the jungle and watching that part of the trail we could see. Behind us, down the line, men were maneuvering and shouting at each other. Higinbotham was superbly cool, talking quietly and easily into the field telephone which was the only link with safety. As long as the artillery held out the Vietnamese could not advance; that was our theory, desperately clung to. Meanwhile the rifle fire got heavier and closer. The bullets were sounding: *Pop!*

Verlumis had left the command post to crawl up the trail toward the heaviest fighting. Pellum Bryant, the senior noncommissioned officer, was below rallying the dozen or so who had fallen under his command. One of the other sergeants was dead. Bryant was the only unwounded man in his eight-man squad. Pinned down by an enfilade of fire, he had huddled in an enemy foxhole. When the fire slackened, he poked up his head and fired bursts. It was Bryant alone who was protecting the rear flank.

By four-thirty in the afternoon, after two hours of fire, the situation was almost lost. The fight had been following a rhythm, with heavy bursts of fire and then silence except for an occasional rattle of a machine gun. The Americans had been pushed back into a tiny area about the size of a basketball court, with Higinbotham and the radio as its nucleus. Bryant was now fighting just a dozen yards to the rear. Hackworth, speaking with Higinbotham, said there was a full company of infantry a mile away. He was ordering them to reinforce.

"You've got to try it," Higinbotham said over the radio. For the first time, his voice cracked and became unsure. There was a 26-year-old advertising account executive or civil servant or department store clerk, or a good old boy at the night baseball game, but not a captain of infantry in the U.S. Army. "If you don't get up here soon, we're all gonna die. If you don't get up here soon, I'm gonna melt."

There was another crackling over the telephone; Hackworth had gone off. Then, barely audibly, but precisely, as if he were reading from a piece of paper, Higinbotham said: "Dear God, please help me save these men's lives."

It got worse after that, and for Higinbotham it was the worst time of all. It was his first patrol with the Tigers. He didn't know the men, either their names or where they came from or how long they had been in Vietnam. Now he had gotten them into this. Higinbotham sat with the radio, his back against a tree, and prayed that it wouldn't be as bad as he thought it was.

The sniper fire came closer, nipping the tops of the branches of the bushes. The artillery seemed to be hitting indiscriminately, as Higinbotham called it closer to the American lines. But there were no lines any more. There was only a group of men huddled silently on a trail that led nowhere down from a ridge line that did not even show on the map. Bryant was on his own, and so was Verlumis. Higinbotham was worried about the artillery, and the tactics were taking care of themselves.

A wounded infantryman, his voice loud as a bullhorn, was calling from the left flank. "You've got to get me out of here!" He was repeating it. The voice was strong and deep, but it cracked with agony and pain. He repeated it again and again. As he screamed and moaned I moved forward. I went forward about five feet and then stopped, still safe. The wounded man was probably twenty yards away, although the jungle was so thick it was impossible to tell. I had the idea that I might save his life.

I looked around at the others and then the wounded man screamed, and was silent. I waited for a minute and then crawled back the five feet. I had spent twenty minutes deciding whether to get the wounded, who had been screaming and pleading for help. Now I didn't have to think about it. He was dead. Verlumis had given me a .45 pistol and now I took it out of its holster for the first time. I was lying on my stomach handling the .45, having dismissed the wounded man from mind. It was easier holding a .45 pistol.

Fifteen yards in front of the command post there was a dip that plunged almost straight down into the ravine. From that direction a voice came: "Airborne!" No one answered. Higinbotham and the radio operator and I looked at the spot where the voice came from. The radioman unhitched a grenade from his ammunition belt, and cradled it like an apple. The voice could belong to anyone, but the odds were better than even that it belonged to a North Vietnamese. I thought of identifying questions to ask. The only two that came to mind was the name of the manager of the New York Yankees, and whether or not Marilyn Monroe was dead or alive. My mind wouldn't work. I thought of asking who wrote the Declaration of Independence, but then figured that a trooper probably wouldn't know the answer. Then I remembered that I didn't know the name of the Yankee manager. Stengel was dead. Or not dead, retired someplace. These thoughts were moving so slowly I could almost see them in my mind's eye. I was closest to the dip and now aimed the pistol straight at it, or just above it. The radioman had not thrown the grenade and all of us were in a state of suspended animation. But then a voice said, "Christ, don't shoot," and a sweat-drenched head appeared over the lip of the ravine. The head belonged to an American.

There were now seven in the command post, and a 360-degree defense. We had been joined by a young rifleman. Still inexplicably careful about journalism, I asked his name; it was Private First Class Sam Washburn, of Indianapolis. Washburn had dived over a bush and told Higinbotham: "I got two Charlies and the captain got one. The captain's dead. We were lying on the trail firing at the Charlies and I looked over and asked him how his ammo was and he was dead." Higinbotham said nothing, did not comment on Verlumis, and continued to talk the artillery in. "I don't think there's anybody else back there," Washburn said. "I mean, any Americans."

That meant that the command post, and the seven of us, *were* the front. There was no protection up the trail. The cries of the wounded were getting louder as the men pulled back into a tighter circle. The command post was filling up with wounded, those who could crawl back or who were carried back by the medics. I would hear only secondhand the horrors endured by the men up the trail; they had been under heavy bombardment for more than three hours. There was no firing from the command post because the enemy could not be seen. But then came the grenades. They were coming closer, just off the mark. That was when the awful fear set in. It was the fear of sudden realization that the North Vietnamese were lobbing grenades and there was no way to stop them.

The faces were all drawn up tight, and there was no talking. A company of reinforcements was on its way, but had got lost. No one knew whether it would arrive in time. Hollow-eyed and distracted, the men moved slowly as in a dream; or perhaps it was me, clammed up and lying flat in that taut circle. In Vietnam if you are thirty years old you feel an old man among youngsters. I was thinking about being thirty, and holding an automatic pistol I didn't know how to fire, when Washburn leaned over and very quietly, very precisely, whispered "grenade." He probably yelled it, but I was switched off, half-deaf from the pounding of the artillery and the

500-pound bombs and it seemed to me that the warning came in a whisper. Then he gave me a push. There was a flash and a furious burst of fire; the grenade had landed a yard away.

I couldn't get my feet down. I was lying on my back, almost standing on my head, and my feet wouldn't come down. Through the numbness and the red haze, I could see Washburn firing, although his hand was blown to pieces, and the radioman using his grenade launcher. Higinbotham was firing, too; but my legs wouldn't come down. Then they were down and I yelled for a medic. "I'm hit!"

"You're OK," Higinbotham said.

"The hell I am," I said. "I'm hit."

"I mean it," he said.

"Christ almighty there's blood everywhere," I said.

"You're all right."

"Goddamnit I'm not."

There was very little pain, just shock and a terrible feeling of relief. I was out of it. The terror was in the knowledge that you might lose control. You had to keep control, and you could feel it slipping away. You were half-crazy looking at the firing. The medic had scrambled up and I called for morphine. My arms and legs were shaking uncontrollably. The medic tackled me and punched the needle into my arm and began to bandage my head and back. The morphine restored the control. My hands and legs were still shaking but I was all right. Higinbotham was grinning. The medic said to take it easy. When the shaking stopped fatigue came.

"You're all right," Higinbotham said.

"I'm not all right, goddamnit," I said.

But we were both laughing, me from shock and Higinbotham from the fact that the attack had been thrown back. The grenades fired by Terry Grey, the radioman, had done it.

"Where are the VC?" I asked.

"We stopped the bastards," Higinbotham said.

I thought that line was in the best MGM tradition, and told Higinbotham so. None of it seemed real, lying in a godforsaken jungle in the middle of a godforsaken war. There were five dead North Vietnamese on the trail a dozen yards away. That was the point of farthest enemy advance. Higinbotham told me of this, and then the firing began once more. He ducked down to work the field telephone and I crawled off beneath a tree as the rat-a-tat-tat of explosions started again. I had lost the pistol and my pack, but I had the camera and my notebook. I thought it would be all right, and anyway I was out of it. There were nineteen wounded men and a dozen dead, and I was one of the wounded. The next two hours were very slow hours. Then the company of reinforcements arrived, crashing through the jungle with banshee whoops and rifle fire.

And that black humorist.

"Where's that newspaper fella?" he asked Higinbotham.

"He got hurt," Higinbotham said.

"Hurt? Sonovabitch."

I thought it would be all right until I saw the helicopters which would take the wounded out; some, like Wills, had lain on the jungle floor for five hours. There was no landing zone, so the helicopters hovered at 100 feet and lowered a T-bar. Strobe lights illuminated the jungle as arc lights illuminate a stadium. The first helicopter took three wounded. A man was strapped onto the T-bar and slowly lifted 100 feet. You ascended alone into the eye of the light, and heard the crack and thwup of bullets, and realized that the enemy, still entrenched on the ridge line, were shooting. They were shooting at the wounded men being pulled into the helicopter. You heard the bullets as you were rising and your body went stiff and you pulled out all the plugs. You gripped the T-bar and made a number of very difficult promises if God got you safely into the helicopter. But when you got there, you said instinctively, I made it. And over and over again, Jesus Christ.

There is no real epilogue to the reconnaissance patrol of the Tiger Force. Its activities that day went unnoticed in the American press because that same afternoon, on a hill only two miles away, Captain William S. Carpenter called napalm on his position after his company had been overrun. Operation Hawthorne, which lasted the better part of a month, was said to be a success. The Americans claimed 1,200 enemy dead, to 250 of their own. In the succeeding twelve months infiltration would continue. Almost eleven months to the day after the opening round of Hawthorne, a battalion of the 173rd Airborne Brigade would get ambushed and badly mauled by a force of North Vietnamese infantry. Lew Higinbotham, who by then had been transferred from the 101st to the 173rd Airborne, was operations officer that day. "How is it?" Higinbotham asked the platoon leader. "Good clean fun," the lieutenant replied. That was at 10 A.M. At ten-twenty the radio went dead; every man in the platoon was killed, or badly wounded. The wire services said the engagement took place a few miles north of Dak To, the Special Forces camp in Kontum province.

7

THE GOOK DOG THAT
HATED GOOKS

MADNESS in Vietnam became infectious, and somehow normal. It was not just the war but the country and the people in the war, both Vietnamese and Americans. The civilians, who were meant to reconstruct the country, had to assume that most Vietnamese were basically friendly; the military, whose business was war, had to conclude that most Vietnamese were basically unfriendly, or at any rate could become unfriendly at the slightest provocation. After a time, a soldier in a hot zone would find conspiracies everywhere. The Vietnamese did not fit into any kind of pattern.

None of it seemed to fit. No one knew who the friendlies were. The friendly was indistinguishable from the unfriendly, unless he had a white face. Then he was a friendly. The American Army ended up fighting the entire country, because it was impossible to tell who was on the right side and who was on the other side. Once in Quang Nam province a Marine platoon was ambushed and nearly wiped out by men dressed in the uniforms of the ARVN infantry. The presumption was that they were Viet Cong. Or was it the reverse? Was the attack an eye for an eye in retaliation for the misdirected artillery fire of the week before? No one knew. The most plausible explanation was that they were Communists dressed as ARVN. But the attack gave the Marines a queer feeling. Late at night frustrated officers at isolated outposts in district towns in Vietnam would talk about razing the entire country. One major thought that all American troops should be pulled out, piled aboard ships, and re-landed at the southern tip of the country, the Camau peninsula, and fight their way north to the Demilitarized Zone just like the landing at Normandy during World War II. Very late at night, after a particularly difficult day, the point was carried further: raze the country and get out; burn it down and start again with Americans. These prescriptions came at the end of a long day, or at the end of a man's tour, when he had been in Vietnam for a year and seen how little had changed, and sensed that nothing very good was happening. The frustrations created their own inner logic, and it happened then that each man had his own Vietnam: the diplomats had one, the generals another, the GI's still another, and the journalists a fourth. There were others as well.

The compulsion was to make no allowances, either in diplomacy or war or journalism. If the facts were straight, the conclusions would be sound. After six months a man had a point of view and clung to it; sometimes the point of view was no view at all, but an abiding faith in confusion and the perversity of the Vietnamese. For the military all of this was most visible in the five northernmost provinces of the country, the I Corps, where the Marines held sway with three divisions. The Marines were forced to fight a conventional war in the I Corps, holding three strong points on the coast and a series of fire bases across the top of the country, just below the Demilitarized Zone. Lacking adequate numbers of helicopters, and surrounded by an unfriendly population, the Marines persisted in an offensive strategy begun seventy years ago in the Caribbean and perfected at Iwo Jima, Tarawa, and Wake. They mounted amphibious assaults on the beaches. These were preceded by barrages from navy cruisers offshore. A battalion of troops, usually fresh from the training camps of Pendleton or Parris Island, assaulted the shore on amtracs (amphibious tractors). There were five of these assaults through the summer of 1967, and none of them was seriously contested by the enemy. There was never any enemy on the beach, and the men rushed inland to find a country of farmers and water buffalo. Marine officials were satisfied that the lack of opposition attested to the success of the seaborne strategy. But as the troops worked inland, the enemy would become more active; when the Marine guard was down, they struck from ambush. This would become increasingly effective as the North Vietnamese perfected their method of fighting from slit trenches and bunkers.

Traditional Marines, and there was scarcely a field-grade Marine officer in Vietnam who was not a traditionalist, liked the strategy of the seaborne assault. It recalled memories of World World II, a war where you were on one side of the line and the enemy was on the other. The seaborne assaults did no positive harm, yet they were symptomatic of the psychology of the American view of the war. Marines had always assaulted from beaches, from Vera Cruz to Iwo Jima. When it was suggested that Vietnam was not Iwo Jima, the Marines would shrug and say it was good practice—for nameless wars in the future.

Of course the seaborne assaults were a minor part of the strategy. The major part involved stanching the flow of troops from the North, keeping the rear areas secure, and sweeping out from the strong points of Phu Bai, Danang and Chu Lai. But Vietnam was a country where the enemy fought at times and places of his own choosing, when he could manage it, and he managed it quite often.

Typical of the problem was the attack of a company of Viet Cong troops on the capital city of Quang Tri province one night in April, 1967. While Viet Cong overran and occupied the city, the ARVN defenders vanished into the night; the enemy rampaged through the streets, freed 250 prisoners from the local jail, struck successfully at two ARVN command posts on the outskirts of town, then as dawn broke marched away into the mountains with the warning that they would be back. Henry L. T. Koren, the senior American civilian in the I Corps, was on the scene the next morning and pronounced the battle as "something out of the Wild West." Koren, a career diplomat who had been ambassador to the Congo (Brazzaville), returned to his villa at Danang that night carrying an M–16 rifle. The ARVN defense was so poor, and the Viet Cong attack so well planned and executed, that American officers were convinced it was an inside job. There was irresistible evidence that one ARVN regimental commander's bodyguard was a Viet Cong agent (the evidence was that he tried to shoot the commander in the back) and there were other, more disquieting reports that were kept secret.

Three days after the attack in Quang Tri, the Marine commander in the I Corps, a sensitive, able and very tough official, spoke of the inability of the Americans to tell the Vietnamese apart, one from the other, to know whom they were fighting, to know whom to trust and whom not to trust. "We can't tell the friendlies from the unfriendlies," said Lieutenant General Lewis W. Walt, "that's *their* job. *They* have to do that. They have got to know who is for them and who is against them. They don't always, and that's just the trouble. But they had better learn."

The I Corps was the scene of the heaviest fighting in the country. By mid-1967 civilian programs had ceased to function and four of the five provinces were very nearly at a state of siege. Apart from massive infiltration characterized as an "invasion" from the North, matters were complicated by political agitation in the city of Hue.

This discontent spread outward and infected villages and hamlets in all the provinces, so on top of the military pressure the Americans had to contend with political upheaval. The pacification program that seemed to be going tolerably well in early 1966 had fallen apart by mid-1967. There was no single explanation: events in the corps went from bad to worse, and American troop reinforcements seemed only to increase the fighting. There was an interesting alternative analysis, which was that stability in the I Corps was always a fiction and that the "collapse" merely reflected reality. It is altogether possible that in 1965 and 1966 the corps was more Communist than it was in 1967, with the guerrilla apparatus so complete that there was no need to mount military offensives; the strategy was simply to wait for the fall of Saigon. The Viet Cong could easily tolerate a few thousand American advisers and the AID representatives, but they could not tolerate 25,000-man divisions. So war erupted, as the Americans realized the nature of the pressure against them. The estimate of the situation in I Corps was so difficult to make that American tactics and strategy became improvisations: if there was no agreement on precisely what the situation was, there could be no agreement on what steps to take to deal with it. It was an impossible position for the American commanders, whose search was not for truth or wisdom but merely for reality. General Walt was vexed and spoke movingly of the complexities, and the need for American patience and endurance. The pessimists, of course, contended that the central fact was not complex at all: most Vietnamese were not, as the Marines insisted, neutral. They were unfriendly. Force of arms sometimes kept them neutral in deed, rarely in thought.

This could never be admitted, despite the evidence, for to admit it would be to say that the Marines were an occupation force. Yet that is what it amounted to. Two years after the Marines landed at Chu Lai and Danang, hamlets around those airfields were considered "insecure." Sniper fire broke out during the day, and the roads were passable only in convoy at night. Intelligence was meager and the government still unable to command the loyalty of village elders, and therefore unable to govern. When a village like Cam Ne proved impossible to pacify, the Marines burned it down; there was, it seemed, no other way. The official view was that the population was indifferent and would give its loyalty and allegiance to whichever force proved able to protect it. Thus was given the picture of a helpless peasantry being pulled to and fro by two opposing forces, one "Free World" and the other "Communist." No doubt this was partly true, but in Vietnam indifference wore many guises and in the I Corps it hid what one American official called "the revolutionary atmosphere." It made Marine efforts all the more futile and almost—feckless. The temptation would be to say two cheers for democracy and let it pass, were the Marines an SS and Walt a Goebbels. But this was not the case. Marine efforts at pacification were extraordinary in their concern for the individual peasant. One young Marine sergeant ponied up $50 of his own money to send a young peasant boy to tailoring school, then contributed another $20 for a bicycle when the youngster complained he had no transport. There were countless examples of kindnesses like this, though the average GI never lost his distrust of the "slopes," as the Orientals were called. There was dedication of the sort personified by Lt. Colonel William B. Corson, an ideosyncratic Marine who intimidated landlords, debated revolutionary theory with Viet Cong agents, brought prosperity to a dozen hamlets around Danang, and generally contributed humor and sophistication to the effort to bring the revolution under Marine control. Corson was not Albert Schweitzer: he did not much care for the Vietnamese, and he was no pacifist humanitarian. But he thought that if the hamlets could be made rich their inhabitants would come to regard the Viet Cong as reactionaries. It was a plausible theory, as plausible as any in South Vietnam, and to a degree it worked. Yet the revolution could not become an American product, and the Vietnamese government still hung back. Pacification did not go forward. It did not move, and under pressure from North Vietnamese troops streaming over the seventeenth parallel and down the Ho Chi Minh trails from Laos in many places, it deteriorated. And Corson, who concluded his tour in the summer of 1967, was pessimistic; he was on the verge of thinking that the war in the I Corps was unwinnable.

So it went slowly. Some said it failed to go at all. But the most important fact was the difficulty of telling the friendlies from the unfriendlies. This was the fact that produced the madness, or the fantasy.

William Tuohy of the Los Angeles *Times* and I came down to Danang from Dong Ha after covering the Marine assault into the Demilitarized Zone in May, 1967. Danang, called Tourane by the French, was the nerve center of the I Corps military establishment, a seaport of narrow streets, indifferent buildings and hostile population. Dong Ha was the forward Marine command post, the locus of seven full American battalions, a gray and uninviting collection of wooden barracks and canvas tents erected on an air strip and radar station about fifteen miles south of the Ben Hai River, the muddy stream that separated North from South Vietnam. About five miles north of the camp was the celebrated "barrier," which looked from the air like a super highway and was supposed to prevent infiltration south from the DMZ. It was surrounded with barbed wire seven miles inland from the sea, and guarded by Marines from bunkers along its edge.

The camp at Dong Ha had been built from practically nothing in mid-1966 to provide the base from which to attack North Vietnamese then entering in strength through the DMZ. The only relic of the old days, when Dong Ha was a radar station, was an air force officers' club, which served good Scotch and had sixteen

Japanese slot machines.* Dong Ha was the end of the world in South Vietnam, in summer hot and dusty and in winter cold and rainy. The scenes there, as the Marines dug in for the heaviest fighting of the war, were reminiscent of the trenches at Verdun or Passchendaele. When it was cold you could stand shivering at the end of the rutted and bumpy air strip and look toward the North Vietnamese mountains, and west toward the mountains bordering Laos. Peasants continued to work the ricefields around the air strip and tiny three-wheeled Lambrettas bussed passengers from Hue, fifty miles to the south, to Gio Linh just below the zone. Gio Linh became important when the Marines decided to emplace .175 mm. guns to reach twenty miles into North Vietnam; then the North Vietnamese emplaced their own guns to reach to Gio Linh and Dong Ha, and there were artillery duels. It was a gray command, gray mud, houses, vehicles, weapons, aircraft, and men. It was a place to stay away from in the best of times, which spring and summer of 1967 were not.

Tuohy and I had been in Dong Ha to report on the battles near the zone, and had by luck been there when the Marines made their first ground assault into it. We arrived after the shooting was over, but there would be three bloody battles in two days, and it looked as if the campaign would continue. We were anxious to return to Saigon to write and file the stories. There was difficulty in getting a military flight to Tan Son Nhut, so on a hunch we went to Air Vietnam, the Vietnamese civilian airline which ran regular schedules

---

* The story of the Vietnam war could be told at Dong Ha. From a quiet air force radar station it went to an armed camp for the Marines, bristling with weapons and fortified buildings, all above ground. When the North Vietnamese brought up their heavy artillery, the camp went underground—or tried to. But the enemy's heavy rockets reached into the bunkers. So in September, 1967, the Marine command decided to relocate farther back, out of range of the guns. The cost in men and material had been high. In the beginning the Marine officers felt, plausibly, that the camp was invulnerable. It was not.

between Danang and Saigon. At the end of the huge airfield there was a filthy terminal and an official and from him we learned there would be a flight that afternoon. So we bought tickets and went into the bar and ordered a drink and sat back to wait the two hours.

It was hot in Danang and the heat brought out the flies, which collected on the sticky beer-stained table. The sun beat through the open windows in full shafts of light, making the room seem even dirtier than it was. There were Vietnamese civilians waiting, and they were seated at places around the windows, guarding children and small bundles and talking quietly. Four ceiling fans whirred and moved the air and the smell was of asphalt and oil and airplane fuel. Across the tarmac were the silver-colored unmarked aircraft of the CIA, ancient C–46's, C–47's, and DC–3's. Some of these same planes had seen duty in China in the 1930's, in Burma and Indochina during World War II, in Korea six years later, and now in Vietnam, Laos and Thailand. They were the symbols of American involvement in Asia and perhaps significantly, perhaps not, the Far East headquarters of Air America, the cover corporation which owned the aircraft, was said to be located at Taiwan. In one country the planes ferried troops, in another food, in a third money, in a fourth drugs. They dropped bulgur wheat and rice to the Montagnards in Vietnam, agents in the North, money in Laos, and weapons in Thailand. Many of the pilots had been in the Far East since the war, collecting danger pay and outrageous stories.

We were drinking beer and watching the planes on the tarmac when two young Marines, an infantryman and an MP, joined us and said they wanted to talk; both were drinking Seagram's whiskey and Coca-Cola and looked as though they had been sitting and drinking most of the afternoon. They were both about nineteen and, in their baggy fatigues, looked pudgy and out of shape.

The private asked us where we had been and when we said Dong Ha he brightened and said that was where he spent most of his time. He had been posted at Dong Ha and now he was going home to California. The private indicated his friend and said that he only had three months to go, and that his job was guarding the slow two-entire transports that took corpses from Danang to Saigon. The planes were loaded at night and he worked an eight-hour shift watching bodies placed aboard the planes. The MP said nothing, sat slouched in his chair, and pulled quietly at the Seagram's and Coke.

The private talked a bit about Dong Ha and his six months there. He said a lot of men had died in and around the zone and the newspapers weren't reporting it. He himself would be twice dead were it not for his dog, Meatball. It had got so in Dong Ha that he would go nowhere without the dog; the entire country was controlled by the Communists (he said this in the same way that zealots speak of the Red Menace in America) and his only protection was the dog.

The problem was in getting the dog back to the United States. The Marines would not permit him to take the dog back because it was a Vietnamese dog, "a gook dog." The private had written to the mayor of Los Angeles, where he lived, and the governor of California, and the two California senators, but had not received replies. Perhaps it was because he did not know the names of these officials. He had addressed the letter to the governor simply:

> Mr. Governor
> California
> USA
> APO San Francisco 96243

since he figured the governor, like everybody else, had an APO number to which letters were sent. Now he was drafting a letter to the President of the United States to secure a release for the dog; the story was so unusual that the President could not fail to respond. There was nothing very special in the breeding, the private said. It was just a mongrel Vietnamese dog.

This was all being said in a low, quiet way, between sips of Seagram's and Coke. The private was being very helpful in supplying specifics, and Tuohy was jotting notes; he thought there might be a story in it for the readers of the Los Angeles *Times: Hollywood GI Bids Help for Hero Dog.*

The private was from Hollywood. The part about the hero dog would come later. He gave Tuohy his street address, which sounded suburban and somehow typical of Southern California. It was a name like Wistful Vista or Twenty-Nine Palms. He said his father was a corporation executive in Los Angeles. The private went on to talk about the difficulty of writing letters to politicians who did not understand the war in Vietnam anyway. It was a disgrace. The trouble with the war was the politicians who ran it.

"We ought to go in there and end it," he said. "end the goddamned war with bombs."

"You know what?" the MP said. "The commandant of the Marine Corps doesn't give a damn what you think."

"It's all right," the private said. "I can have my own opinions."

The friend snorted. "And it doesn't make any difference."

"Well, at least they ought to take care of the dog."

"Tell us about the dog," Tuohy said.

The private was twisting a matchbook in his hand, and put it down and picked up his drink. Meatball was no ordinary gook dog, he said. For one thing, it was a dog that hated Vietnamese and loved Americans. "That dog loved us Marines and hated the gooks," the private said. "He hated the gooks and would do anything to get them; all he had to do was see a gook, and he would begin to growl; I had to restrain him, go around with him on a leash or he would attack." The dog was an ordinary mongrel, which he had got from a friend who died. It knew about the Vietnamese because it was Vietnamese. "It takes one to know one," the private said.

The dog, in fact, was a hero of sorts. Twice he saved patrols from ambush. The first time, Meatball braved enemy fire to scurry back to the command post to bring forward bandoliers of ammunition; the second time he barked and disclosed the position of a sniper. For that he had been wounded. "Meatball can smell gooks a mile away," said the private. "When he smells them, he barks."

Tuohy wanted to hear more about the bandoliers and the wounding. The private ordered a Seagram's and Coke for himself and the MP, and two beers for Tuohy and me. He had taken off the battered Marine fatigue cap, and now he scratched his head thoughtfully.

"We were pinned down under fire at night," the private said. "And I ran out of ammunition, and the dog went all the way back to the CP and got the bandoliers and brought them back. We had cleared out the gooks by then but Meatball was great. He got hit by some sort of fragment in the leg. He did a lot of crawling on his belly." The private had been staring across the room and I followed his eyes. He was looking at a Vietnamese man who had an enormous growth on the back of his head. It was as big as a grapefruit. "Meatball is in the hospital now," the private went on, "with some sort of growth. It looks sort of like that gook over there." He pointed across the room.

He wanted to take the dog back to the United States but the authorities were forbidding it. He wanted to do it legally, no matter how many forms there were to fill out, or how many letters there were to write; you got used to red tape in the Marine Corps—"the right way, the wrong way, and the Marine Corps way," the private said. But if he could not he would do it illegally. He would not leave Vietnam without the dog. You wouldn't either, if you knew how terrible life in Dong Ha was; the dog was what made it bearable. He began to talk after a while of life in Dong Ha, and what it was like on the patrols that moved out from camp at dusk and did not return until dawn.

You never knew where you were and you never knew where the enemy was. There was only the darkness and the rain forests, and the heat of the ricefields. The country looked the same from one field to another. He had patrolled the same fields, sometimes at night and sometimes during the day. It was dangerous either way. Nothing happened on most of the patrols, so the men got careless. The lines bunched up and the rule of silence was broken; or there was a new CO who didn't know the score. The platoon leaders would curse and rail at the men, but after a certain number of patrols when nothing happened and there was only the heat and the limitless green of the ricefields the men ceased to pay attention. Then a booby trap would go off or a sniper kill or wound a man and the platoon would reform into a careful unit. In the afternoon you would be listening to the Tijuana Brass on a transistor radio, and in the evening be scared to death in the middle of a ricefield, watching the tree line and hoping nobody was there. In the morning you would be back with the Tijuana Brass. It was worse when the Vietnamese went along on the patrol, as scouts or in the combined action platoons. You never knew what was going to happen, or when. You never knew if the Vietnamese were going to desert, run back to their own lines, or perhaps work with the Viet Cong. Maybe they were the Viet Cong. None of the American troops spoke Vietnamese so you could never be sure what they were saying. And the interpreters didn't speak English, no matter what the CO said. It was a place where the enemy was everywhere. Then it really was a jungle and you had to be doubly alert.

All of this was endurable with Meatball, the gook dog. Meatball, being a gook, knew all about gooks, could smell them and smoke them out wherever they were. When a patrol went out with gooks, Meatball went along as insurance. He was kept on a loose leash, and everyone including the platoon leader was glad he was there; and he proved it twice, saving the platoon from disaster. Of course, the gooks themselves didn't like it, weren't happy about it, and some of them complained. But the dog was part of the platoon.

"How did he get the name Meatball?"

"It's just a name," the private said, "like any name."

While the private talked, I watched the tarmac and now saw an ancient Dakota transport with Air Vietnam markings easing into a berth in front of the terminal. I walked outside and verified it was the plane for Saigon. It was brutally hot on the asphalt runway, and I paused under the wing to look over the field and its burden of jet fighters, four-engine transports, and at the far end a Pan American jet loading Marines bound for Rest and Recreation in Okinawa or home. One of the unmarked planes was being loaded with a mysterious cargo by its civilian crew. I was standing in the heat and looking at the planes when I felt a tap on my shoulder. It was the MP.

"You know I'm taking him to Saigon," the MP said, motioning to the terminal where the private was still talking with Tuohy.

I nodded and asked what the trouble was.

"Maybe you noticed that I am carrying a weapon, and he isn't."

I hadn't noticed, but it was true. The MP was carrying a .45 pistol without the clip. The private had no weapon. The MP smiled and said almost apologetically that the private was a loony, and had gotten loose in Danang and had gone to Dong Ha. He had disappeared for six weeks. No one knew what he had done in Dong Ha, how he had gotten there and how he managed to evade the MP's. But he was found, arrested and taken into custody. The private was a loony, the MP went on, a troublemaker. There was no dog named Meatball, and no letters to the mayor of Los Angeles, the governor of California, or the President of the United States.

"You better tell your friend this, before he writes it up for his newspaper," the MP said.

I said I was glad to know it, and thanked the MP.

"You don't have to worry about him or anything," he said. "He's not violent. He won't cause no trouble."

We went inside and the private was still talking about the dog and the difficulty of getting it to Los Angeles. He was telling the whole story over again. Tuohy was no longer taking notes, just sitting and listening to the private.

"You know something?" the MP said.

"No," the private said.

"The commandant doesn't give a damn about your dog, either."

"I know that," the private said.

"Well, why do you keep talking about it?"

The private shrugged and the MP said they were going. Everyone shook hands all around and wished luck. The two walked out of the airport bar very slowly, the MP behind and slightly to the rear of the private.

PublicAffairs is a new nonfiction publishing house and a tribute to the standards, values, and flair of three persons who have served as mentors to countless reporters, writers, editors, and book people of all kinds, including me.

I.F. STONE, proprietor of *I. F. Stone's Weekly*, combined a commitment to the First Amendment with entrepreneurial zeal and reporting skill and became one of the great independent journalists in American history. At the age of eighty, Izzy published *The Trial of Socrates*, which was a national bestseller. He wrote the book after he taught himself ancient Greek.

BENJAMIN C. BRADLEE was for nearly thirty years the charismatic editorial leader of *The Washington Post*. It was Ben who gave the *Post* the range and courage to pursue such historic issues as Watergate. He supported his reporters with a tenacity that made them fearless and it is no accident that so many became authors of influential, best-selling books.

ROBERT L. BERNSTEIN, the chief executive of Random House for more than a quarter century, guided one of the nation's premier publishing houses. Bob was personally responsible for many books of political dissent and argument that challenged tyranny around the globe. He is also the founder and longtime chair of Human Rights Watch, one of the most respected human rights organizations in the world.

———

For fifty years, the banner of Public Affairs Press was carried by its owner Morris B. Schnapper, who published Gandhi, Nasser, Toynbee, Truman and about 1,500 other authors. In 1983, Schnapper was described by *The Washington Post* as "a redoubtable gadfly." His legacy will endure in the books to come.

Peter Osnos, *Publisher*